FIRST EDITION

WHAT COLOR ARE YOUR JELLYBEANS?

INTERSECTIONS OF GENERATION, RACE, SEX, CULTURE, AND GENDER

By **Felecia Carter Harris, Ed.D.**

UNIVERSITY OF NORTH CAROLINA - CHARLOTTE

cognella®
academic publishing

Bassim Hamadeh, CEO and Publisher

Kassie Graves, Director of Acquisitions

Jamie Giganti, Senior Managing Editor

Jess Estrella, Senior Graphic Designer

Mieka Portier, Senior Acquisitions Editor

Sean Adams, Project Editor

Luiz Ferreira, Senior Licensing Specialist

Christian Berk, Associate Editor

Kat Ragudos, Interior Designer

Printed in the United States of America

ISBN: 978-1-5165-1246-1 (pb) / 978-1-5165-1247-8 (br)

www.cognella.com   800-200-3908

CONTENTS

ACKNOWLEDGEMENTS

"Commit to the Lord whatever you do, and he will establish your plan."

PROVERBS 16:3.

Writing a book is not an easy task coupled with being a wife, mother, professor and other obligations, it would be impossible without GOD directing my path, and the support and encouragement of family members, friends, colleagues and editors. I owe thanks to many.

I would like to thank my husband Ken for his love, support, patience and encouragement throughout the development and completion of this project. Thanks also to my children Sydney and Christian for your enthusiasm about mom being an author.

Many thanks to Monique Mckenzie Brown for initially putting my words to paper and Cama McNamera for the countless hours you spent editing the manuscript and pushing me to finally finish this book.

Many thanks also to the team at Cognella publishing, Mieka, Sean, Dani, and Jess. You all went above and beyond, in a very short period of time to help me complete this wonderful book.

I wrote this book because I wanted to help people understand and learn the value we all have; we just present it in different ways. It is those differences that make us all valuable and unique. So I acknowledge you, the reader, for joining me in this journey.

"Diversity: verb - To expand your outlook and network"
—*CHARREAH K. JACKSON*

"How good and pleasant it is when brothers live together in unity."
—*PSALM 133:1*

PREFACE

I began writing this book several years ago under the assumption that we live in a post-racial, post-generational America. Our neighborhoods and churches are integrated; baby boomers work cooperatively with Millennials; Hispanic, Arabic, and Asian children sit beside African Americans and Whites in the classroom; interracial couples no longer draw stares; and, according to recent studies, young children are more concerned about whether a person is nice than the color of his skin.

Although my grandmother recalls stories of the bias and hate she endured throughout much of her life, my students at the University of North Carolina at Charlotte often wonder why I teach a class that, among other topics, focuses on racism, colorblindness, and stereotypes. Most African Americans born in the late 1990s have no serious personal references for racial discrimination, although many have experienced unpleasant encounters, such as being questioned by authorities if they seemed out of place in particular areas of town or in certain situations, or being followed around in stores as if they were shoplifters.

Yes, we thought our nation was moving forward from its racially divided past, but we began to notice that things were changing—or perhaps nothing had changed at all—when a string of violent incidents caught our attention. The first one occurred in 2012 in Sanford, Florida, where Trayvon Martin, an unarmed Black teenager, was shot and killed by the White neighborhood watch captain, George Zimmerman. In August 2014 the town of Ferguson, Mississippi, erupted in violence after 18-year-old Michael Brown, an unarmed Black man, was shot and killed by a White police officer; and in North Charleston, South Carolina, in April 2015 50-year-old Walter Scott was stopped by a White police officer for having a broken taillight. The scene turned violent when the unarmed Scott fled, and the officer, Michael Slager, shot him in the back.

These are but a few of the events that have occurred over the past few years between Black men and armed White men, but the racial divide doesn't end there. Despite the fact that many of my students have a naïve attitude toward racism, college campuses often mirror mainstream society. The University of Oklahoma Kappa chapter of Sigma Alpha Epsilon was shut down in March 2015 after members were filmed singing racial slurs on a bus. Eight months later, hundreds of students at the University of California, Los Angeles protested after some students wore blackface to a Kanye West–themed fraternity party. And the country was shocked in November 2015 when President Tim Wolfe and Chancellor R. Bowen Loftin stepped down from their positions at the University of Missouri after they came under fire for the mishandling of racism on campus. As disturbing as these incidents are, they are nothing new. In 2015 the U.S. Department of Education recorded 146 cases of racial harassment on college and university campuses, down from 177 in 2014 but up from 96 in 2009.

The violence and hatred in our society crosses lines other than color. In August 2012 a massacre took place at the Sikh temple in Oak Creek, Wisconsin, where six temple members were gunned down by White supremacist Wade Michael Page; and in February 2015 three Muslim students, Deah Shaddy Barakat, his wife, Yusor Mohammad Abu-Salha, and her sister, Razan Mohammad Abu-Salha, were shot and killed by Craig Stephen Hicks, a White man, in Chapel Hill, North Carolina.

Then there was an event so tragic it became a rallying cry for people of all races, colors and religions: Emanuel. Dylann Roof, a 21-year-old White man, joined a prayer circle at Emanuel African Methodist Episcopal Church in Charleston, South Carolina, and proceeded to shoot 10 African American members, killing nine, in an effort to foment racial tension across the country.

No matter how hard we want to believe that we see each other as equals, racial and ethnic biases in our society are pervasive. In our own defense, stereotyping and discriminating often occur without the offender realizing it is happening—mainly because of a lack of cultural awareness or understanding.

Let's take a look at a few more examples:

- Asian American Jeremy Lin electrified NBA fans in 2012 as he led a winning streak as point guard for the New York Knicks, creating a global phenomenon known as "Linsanity." As the first American of Chinese descent to play in the NBA, Lin's presence on the court highlighted racial profiling in sports. The Harvard University graduate overcame the stereotype that Asians are smart but cannot play basketball (Gregory, 2012).
- Culinary mogul and TV chef Paula Deen was fired from the Food Network for admitting that she privately condoned racist jokes and used the N-word. In a public apology defending her attitude toward race Deen stated, "We're all prejudiced against one thing or another. I think Black people feel the same prejudice as White people feel" (Moskin, June 21, 2013, New York Times p. B1; Dennis, July 8, 2013, p.1).
- The N-word, although trivialized and more mainstreamed than ever, is still a racially offensive term. Its usage has been blurred by the entertainment industry in platforms such as poetry, literature, music, comedy, movies, and sports, so we ask ourselves: Who can say the N-word? When can it be used and in what context? Unfortunately, the N-word is not going away anytime soon, and its generational and historical baggage will not change (Taylor, 2013).

- One of the most publicized debacles of a sports figure during the writing of this project was that of former Los Angeles Clippers' owner Donald Sterling, who made offensive racist remarks that were recorded. The story broke when the recording was shared by TMZ. It then spread like wildfire for the world to hear. Even though every American is entitled to express one's views through First Amendment rights, sometimes it pays to keep one's thoughts to oneself. Sterling was not only the first NBA team owner to lose his team over bigoted remarks; his words also cost him $2.5 million in fines.

The previous examples demonstrate that racism, prejudice, and a lack of respectfully acknowledging differences still operate in a society that explicitly and publicly condemns them. Why? Various manifestations are cleaned up, streamlined, and mainstreamed—which allows them to survive (Winant, 2007).

During the completion of this book, I had the opportunity to sit down and talk with one of my colleagues at UNC-Charlotte, Dr. Shannon Sullivan, the author of *Good White People*. Although Dr. Sullivan's book is not strictly focused on differences, she does examine the intersection of race, class, privilege, and how cultural and educational capital position individuals—especially White people—at the top. She takes a look at how simply being White impacts how differences are acknowledged, not acknowledged, or included in conversations about race.

What Color Are Your Jellybeans? explores how issues dealing with differences like race, culture, and generation are either examined in isolation, overlooked, or not discussed in public at all. Similarly, *Good White People* puts a name on something that is usually not said out loud. For example, White people are not really racists. She says that White people don't think of themselves as White, and they surely are not surrounded by racists. However, if someone is racist, it is those "other people," not themselves. According to Dr. Sullivan, by identifying themselves as White but also slipping in the word "good," the label acknowledges there is a difference between the "good" ones and the "bad" ones.

To show that you're not a racist has become synonymous with showing your class status: You don't say certain things, and you don't talk about race openly. Also, saying some of these things out loud may make White people—as well as other groups—uncomfortable. There's a set of conversations about race and class in the United States that White people have only begun to have, and maybe don't even understand how to have.

These conversations must start with being accurately educated about differences. We are not born with stereotypes, prejudices, or racism. However, learning these attitudes begins early. Even in our preschool years we are exposed to misinformation or no information at all. If we live in communities without diversity, we may have limited opportunities to learn about it the right way.

Dr. Sullivan further explains that kids' conversations can teach us a lot, although kids very quickly learn and pick up subtle cues from adults. They notice what adults are and aren't talking about, and what they're uncomfortable talking about. What we learn is from them is who we are. In the same ways we learn those perceptions and actions, we must learn how to do it right. *What Color Are Your Jellybeans?* is the first step (S. Sullivan, interview, January 20, 2016).

Despite the diversity surrounding us, the decisions about who we allow in our personal spaces are also impacted by hot topics surrounding race, which have the potential to set people off. For example, using the term "colorblind" has become synonymous with acknowledging "I do not see color" (race), therefore I value everyone the same. According to Tim Wise (2010), in his book *Colorblind: The Rise of Post-Racial Politics and the Retreat From Racial Equity*, our ability to tackle or even openly discuss matters relevant to race remains a challenge. Having open discussions that are not just "colorblind" but also acknowledge the various ways in which we experience society around us is important in understanding each other and building relationships.

Developing exceptional relationships is about the accuracy of the information you receive and how you react to it. As you read the contents of this book, keep in mind that our differences should be used to build relationships rather than divide us. Making connections with others is what makes all of us human and allows us to remain hopeful in our daily interactions as we encounter people who are as different as the colors of jellybeans.

"You are only an attitude away from success!"
— *JOHN C. MAXWELL*

"Examining differences or racism is not about how you look, it is about how people assign meaning to how you look."
— *ROBIN D.G. KELLY, HISTORIAN.*

INTRODUCTION

"IT'S A SMALL WORLD AFTER ALL"

....

"You can tell a lot about a fellow's character by the way he eats jellybeans."

— *PRESIDENT RONALD REAGAN*

You might ask, what do jellybeans have to do with building extraordinary relationships? Unless you're a Jelly Belly looking for a soul mate, the concept might seem farfetched. On the other hand, I've spent the last two decades researching interpersonal relationships and have concluded that there is no simpler way to represent the variety of people on our great planet. Jellybeans come in a variety of shapes, colors, textures, and sizes—just as we do. If used effectively, they can reveal how well we interact with the people around us—and indicate changes necessary to improve those interactions.

I began using jellybeans in presentations on professional development, diversity, and inclusion for business owners, government agencies, corporate executives, and nonprofit and educational organizations. Before the participants arrived, I took a handful of a single color of jellybeans and placed them in individual clear cups labeled with various racial and ethnic groups. For example:

- White American or Caucasian
- African American or Black
- Native American
- Asian
- Pacific Islander
- Latino
- Hispanic
- European
- African
- Australian
- Other

These labels were not inclusive of every individual global group because of the sheer number of cups, but those represented provided participants with numerous selections and the opportunity to add additional identifiers if necessary. Each participant received an empty clear cup and was asked to select a jellybean from one of the labeled cups that best represented their answers to a series of questions. These related to a variety of personal, professional, and leisure activities. For example: What was the race or ethnic background of the last person(s) you had lunch with? Participants placed a jellybean representative of the various races or ethnicities of the people with whom they had eaten lunch in their cups.

Another question concerned neighbors: Do you know the cultural backgrounds of the people who live in close proximity to your home? The participants continued to put relevant jellybeans in their cups. I also asked about the cultural background of the author(s) of the most recent book(s) the participants had read. Another question was: How many different cultural groups were represented at the last personal or professional gathering you attended?

I used the same process to examine generational differences. Cups were labeled "Traditionalist," "Baby Boomer," "Generation Xer," "Millennial," and "Generation Zer," and jellybeans of a particular color were placed in the cups in answer to my questions. For example:

- To what generational group(s) did the individual(s) you had lunch with last week belong?
- How many different generational groups were represented at the last personal or professional gathering you attended? What were they?
- What is the generation(s) of the characters in your favorite television programs?

After all the questions were completed, I asked participants to observe the colors of the jellybeans they had collected. Most were surprised and somewhat ashamed by the lack of variety. Many realized for the first time how little contact they had on a daily basis with people who were different from them racially, culturally, and generationally.

Social psychologist Dr. Jennifer Richeson, a MacArthur Genius Award recipient, also uses jellybeans to bring home her discussions on stereotypes and prejudice. "I really like jellybeans—especially green jellybeans," she says. "I could eat myself sick—and I do," she tells the students in her course. If she were to pick only one jellybean from a pack, it would probably be green, but if she were to scoop up a handful, she wouldn't put the other colors back "because it's rude and because it just doesn't seem right. It's called a variety pack for a reason."

Taking jellybeans one at a time, you can easily fail to realize that you favor a single color. See all your green selections at once, though, and it's obvious. The anecdote relates to what she tells her students: "If you want to understand stereotypes and prejudice, and how people often deal with difference—don't just look at conscious thoughts and spoken words, but at what people feel and do without realizing it."

The jellybean exercise reveals how much emphasis we place on visual differences. I have learned over the years that we spend a lot of time thinking about how we can develop relationships in the most comfortable of ways, not understanding how this limits our options. Instead, we need to focus on how we can better educate ourselves to develop diverse relationships.

When you give someone an opportunity to interact with you without either of you wearing blinders, you learn about them—and from them—and despite your differences, you may be surprised at how well you get along. Making room to enjoy new relationships can help you recognize that everyone has innate value and should be shown respect.

THE MESSAGE

So let's say the jellybeans in your cup are just as uniform as those of the participants in the exercise. What does this mean for you? It means that you may have limited those you associate with to a very small group, and in the process are preventing yourself from experiencing the gifts that people from other groups or cultures have to offer. More important, you are not making your gifts and talents available to others. I wrote this book because I believe that everyone must seize the opportunity to value the differences in others. By doing so, we can take advantage of the diversity in cultures, skills, education, talents, innovation, and religion that surround us.

As an educator, trainer, and consultant, I have experienced the struggles, frustration, and anguish that individuals and organizations face when diversity and differences surface as challenges. Issues surrounding this topic are often discussed or debated in personal circles, but they continue to remain a subject most people are uncomfortable examining in public.

THE DESIGN

This interactive guide is designed to help individuals and organizations attain more fulfilling, beneficial, and diverse relationships. Why is this important?

An organization will never reach its full potential if only a certain type of employee is hired. To be innovative, a company needs workers with a variety of perspectives on challenges and solutions. This requires a diverse workforce in regard to age, race, gender, and culture.

If you never step outside of your cultural comfort zone, you miss out on the ability to enjoy other people's creativity, perceptions, innovation, and conversations. Such conversations will assist you in creating perceptions that are based on facts rather than myths, which are difficult to overcome and lead to incorrect assumptions. According to Antonio Damasio, professor of neuroscience at the University of Southern California and an adjunct professor at the Salk Institute, there are biological reasons we recognize differences, but many of our responses are created by our own perceptions of a situation (Johnson, 2011).

Dr. Jill Taylor's groundbreaking book, *My Stroke of Insight*, which explores the process of rebuilding her brain to connect with the world after having a stroke, further explains that we recognize differences through our limbic system. This system mediates how we process information through our senses and controls how we perceive incoming information. The limbic system allows us to scan incoming information in an immediate moment and determine if it is OK to proceed. For any two people to communicate with one another they must share a certain amount of common reality (Taylor, 2006). Developing comfort and a sense a familiarity allows the brain to feel we can safely connect with people who are different and can expose us to new friendships, foods, recreational activities, religions, and social interactions.

This book is based on the following core questions:

1. Why and how do we choose to develop the relationships we do?
2. What gets in the way of exploring those relationships outside our natural/normal circle of people or comfort zone?
3. What experiences can happen when you choose to explore and learn about new people? No matter in which part of the globe you live, understanding how we educate ourselves about those who are different can be life changing. In order to examine this process we will discuss issues related to race, ethnicity, gender, generations, and communication. It truly is a small world after all.

WHAT'S INSIDE?

- Chapter 1, *Skin Deep*, introduces the jellybean exercise as we explore your interactions on a basic level. We'll look at the types of people you choose to interact with on a consistent basis.
- Chapter 2, *I See Colored People*, focuses on the consequences of not actively seeking relationships with people who are different.
- Chapter 3, *We're All a Little Weird*, explores whether anyone is really "normal."
- Chapter 4, *Dare to Be Different*, discusses the impact of stereotypes and myths, and what we can learn once we have factual information.
- Chapter 5, *Judge Not*, acknowledges that our natural instinct is to judge but explains how judging keeps us from learning from each other.
- Chapter 6, *Can't We All Just Get Along?*, reveals we must move past personal barriers if we want to change the way we think and interact with people who are different from us.
- Chapter 7, *Lost in Translation*, analyzes the complexities of communication and cultural dimensions, and discusses how our fears get in the way.
- Chapter 8, *Always Connected; Never in Touch*, explores the impact of digital technology.

- Chapter 9, *When You Know Better*, You Do Better, shows how educating yourself is the best way to understand and value differences.
- Chapter 10, *Just Do It!*, examines the personal fulfillment you can expect to attain by opening your mind and expanding your network of friends and acquaintances, one person at a time.
- Chapter 11, *Commit to Long-Term Change!*, wraps it all up with 50 steps to take action right now.

Are you ready to embark on this journey in your personal development? Of course you are. Pack away your inhibitions, stereotypes, misconceptions, and fears, and get ready for transformation.

FIVE GENERATIONS

CAN YOU RELATE?

In this day and age, it is imperative that you can relate not only to people of other races and cultures but also to those with varied ideas and attitudes. The five major generations within our current population include:

- **Traditionalists (born 1922–1943):** These hard workers are recognized for their conformity and ability to receive delayed rewards. They are conservative dressers, save their money, and pay cash for purchases. Many grew up during the Great Depression. During their lifetime, Social Security was established, World War II was fought, the atomic bomb was dropped, and Mickey Mouse was created. Traditionalists grew up in the era of radio, Tarzan, and the introduction of Wheaties. Traditionalists get their information from *Reader's Digest*, the *Wall Street Journal*, and *Time*.
- **Baby Boomers (born 1943–1964):** These optimists seek personal growth and gratification. They are workaholics and are involved in their communities. During their lifetime, President John F. Kennedy was elected, the Peace Corps was established, Martin Luther King, Jr. marched on Washington, the National Organization for Women was created, the first nuclear power plant was built, the Vietnam War was fought, Woodstock happened, and cellular phones were introduced. In addition, President Kennedy, Martin Luther King, Jr., and Robert F. Kennedy were assassinated. Baby Boomers grew up watching the *Ed Sullivan Show* and eating TV dinners, and made the peace sign, hula hoops, and designer glasses popular. *People* magazine and *Business Week* are favorite reads.
- **Generation Xers (born 1960–1980):** This generation is one of diversity and global thinking. Gen Xers are adaptable, self-reliant, independent, and technoliterate. They experienced the Women's Liberation Movement, Watergate, Three Mile Island, the Challenger Disaster, Ronald Reagan's presidency, the fall of the Berlin Wall, and the Rodney King beating. Xers grew up with the

The Brady Bunch, platform shoes, Cabbage Patch dolls, nose rings, tattoos, and chat rooms. *Dynasty* and *The Simpsons* were popular television shows.

- **Millennials/Nexters (born 1980–2000):** This child-focused generation is experiencing busy, over-planned lives and stress, although it is optimistic, confident, and diverse. Millennials have been affected by the Oklahoma City Bombing, the Columbine High School massacre, 9/11, and the advance of technology. Popular during this generation's childhood were Barney, Beanie Babies, American Girl dolls, Oprah, the Spice Girls, Michael Jordan, Princess Diana, Bill Gates, Tiger Woods, Mia Hamm, and *Goosebumps*.

- **Generation Zers (born 1994–2004):** This generation, which lives in an almost virtual world, is in a stage of evolution. Known as the "silent generation" because its members are so connected digitally, Zers are poor communicators and lack interpersonal skills. They are accustomed to instant action, satisfaction, and immediate results. Zers' primary means of communication is through Google, Facebook, and MySpace. They do not meet their friends face-to-face and are less likely than other generations to travel or step out of their homes for anything. Zers are individualistic, believe men and women are equal, live very structured lives, and speak their minds and express opinions through the digital community.

REFERENCES

McCrindle, M., & Wolfinger, E. (2009). *The ABC of XYZ: Understanding the global generations*. New South Wales: UNSW Press.

Zemke, R., Raines, C., & Filipczak, B. (2000). *Generations at work: Managing the clash of veterans, Boomers, Xers, and Nexters in your workplace*. New York: American Management Association.

CHAPTER 1

SKIN DEEP

· ·

> "Their skin may be different from yours,
> and their homes maybe different from yours.
> Their schools may be different from yours,
> and their lands may be different from yours.
> Their lives may be different from yours,
> and their words may be different from yours.
> But inside, their hearts are just like yours,
> whoever they are, wherever they are, all over the world."

— FROM THE CHILDREN'S BOOK WHOEVER YOU ARE, BY MEM FOX

Imagine for a moment that you pulled back all the layers of your skin. What would you see? Through the international science exhibit Gunther von Hagens's Body Worlds, now in its 11th year of touring, you would notice that all human beings look alike underneath this vital but often divisive organ. As much as people differ in body type, shape, height, and size, all human beings look alike when their outer layers are removed. Without skin as a point of reference, biases, assumptions, and judgments are harder to establish.

Why are we so challenged by other people's differences? Why do these minute differences prevent us from connecting with people who do not look like us? The answers are as varied as the people on earth.

If we could reduce the world's population of 7 billion to a village of precisely 100 people, with all existing human ratios remaining the same, and keeping in mind that each of the villagers represents 70 billion people, the demographics would look something like this:

Half of the villagers would be female; the other half would be male. Eight villagers would be 65 years of age and older, while 26 would be under the age of 14. The estimated life span would be 67.59 years.

The largest number of contingents—61—would be natives of China, India, and Africa. The continent of Europe would be represented by 10 villagers. Nine villagers would be of South American and

Caribbean descent. Only five villagers would come from North America, one of whom would be the president of the United States.

As you walked through the village, you would hear Mandarin, as well as Spanish, English, Hindi, and Bengali. You would also notice Arabic, Portuguese, Russian, Japanese, and German.

Religions would include Christianity, Islam, Buddhism, Hinduism, Shintoism, and Judaism. A few people in the village would be atheists, and at least five would identify as lesbian or gay.

What about living conditions? Twenty-five villagers would reside in substandard housing or have no home at all. Forty would lack access to basic sanitation, and 13 would not have safe drinking water. Eighty-two villagers would be from less developed countries, with an average income of $5,440 a year— or the equivalent of $15 per day.

Fifty villagers would rely on coastal habitats for food sources. Twenty-two would be overweight, and 13 would suffer from malnutrition. One villager would have HIV/AIDS—the equivalent of 70 million people infected. Ten people would be unemployed. Those with jobs would mainly work in agriculture, industry, and services.

Seven villagers would have a college education, but seven would be unable to read or write.

Technology, of course, would be available in the village. Seventy-seven mobile phones would be unequally distributed, with some villagers possessing two or more; others would have none. Thirty-three villagers would use the Internet, with 15 having Internet access in their homes. Twelve would be active participants on Facebook.

The extremely wealthy would come from Europe, the United States, India, and Asia. The richest individual would own 40 percent of the village's entire wealth (FCF, 2011).

When you consider our world from such an incredibly compressed perspective, the need for cooperation, understanding, and tolerance becomes even more evident. Broadening your relationships will not only enhance your personal development; it will boost your career and economic development as well. But there's more to this story. If you think that redesigning your intercultural relationships is just a feel-good exercise, think again.

We live on a globally diverse planet that seems to grow smaller daily. China, the world's largest country, has a population of 1.3 billion; while the second largest, India, has a mere 100,000 fewer citizens. Although the United States, ranked third, has an estimated 3.2 million residents, the face of America is changing quickly. Minorities, classified by the U.S. Census Bureau as those of any race other than non-Hispanic, single-race Whites, currently constitute about one-third of the U.S. population. By 2042 the Bureau projects that the minority will become the new majority, comprising more than one-half of the population. By 2050 that number is expected to increase to 54 percent.

Minority children are projected to reach that milestone even sooner. By 2023 the U.S. Census Bureau estimates that more than one-half of all children will be considered minorities.

Another telling statistic: The percentage of the U.S. population between the ages of 18 and 64—the "working-age" population in 1978 this population was 130 million and has risen to 210 million in 2016 (US Census Data). However this population—is projected to decrease to 57 percent in 2050. The workforce will change as it incorporates a new working-age population that is more than 30 percent Hispanic; as well as 15 percent African-American, and 9.6 percent Asian. The number of residents older than 65 will more than double, making it more important than ever to plan for and appreciate an aging population.

So the winds of change are upon us. It becomes more important each day for each of us to determine that the human experience isn't about how different we are, but how similar we are, and acknowledge the benefits of our shared experiences.

"The minority population will account for more than 90 percent of the total growth of the U.S. population through 2050."
—*U.S. CENSUS BUREAU*

MY THOUGHTS AND OBSERVATIONS

_____

_____

_____

_____

_____

_____

_____

_____

_____

_____

_____

_____

CHAPTER 2

I SEE COLORED PEOPLE

● ●

"The greatest discovery of my generation is that a human
being can alter his life altering his attitudes."

— *WILLIAM JAMES*

The title of this chapter, *I See Colored People*, is a play off the quote "I see dead people" from the movie *The Sixth Sense*. The film, starring Bruce Willis and Haley Joel Osment, chronicles how Osment's character, Cole Sear, communicates with spirits who don't realize they are dead. The audience is completely drawn into the conversations that take place between Sear and his psychologist, Dr. Malcolm Crowe, Willis's character. It is not until the end of the movie that the audience, completely mesmerized by the chilling exchange between the two, realizes Crowe is also dead.

How many times have we made assumptions about people, only to discover we have much to learn? "I do not see color" is a line I often hear from people of various cultural groups when they find out I do diversity work. I immediately ask them, "What does that mean?" They respond, "I'm colorblind. I don't make distinctions among people of different races. All people are the same to me."

I have also had individuals say proudly, "I know Black people, Asians, and Latinos." While some people may brag about their ability to see through color or the fact that they know people from other countries, I don't necessarily view these as positive comments. There is no way that you can look at me and not notice that I'm an African American female. To say "I don't see color" means that you don't see me.

Seeing differences in skin color is not a problem, but using colorblind language to justify or verify we all are exactly the same is. For those who feel they know me because they have made the acquaintance of other Black people, I say that each of us—no matter the color of our skin—is unique; it's our talents and cultural imprints that make us who we are.

Using a colorblind perspective is not as simplistic as it appears, although it has become commonplace. Over the last two decades, mass media and technology have allowed us to view various cultural or ethnic groups, customs, races, and pop culture in the workplace or in our homes without the benefit of having experienced them in the context in which they originated.

The distinction of racial and ethnic differences has historically been rooted in biology. Such characteristics as head size or skin color have been used to maintain cultural boundaries. The use of the word "colorblind" makes the character of social relationships difficult to identify and eliminates the consideration of race and cultural differences, which ignores who people really are (Collins, 2005). As a result it:

- Provides no space for bona fide differences
- Contains issues of cultural differences and race "safely" in a box
- Allows cultural groups to be seen but not heard
- Avoids overt verbal expression of race and culture
- Eliminates the opportunity to highlight individual and community uniqueness
- Refuses to acknowledge the social experiences of race and culture
  (Bonilla-Silva, 2006, pp. 3; 55–57)

In essence, using race-neutral language, like the term "colorblind," has the opposite effect. It nullifies your actual meaning. Racial, cultural, or ethnic differences will always exist among us. Being conscious of our differences acknowledges that humans have the capacity to show care and concern for others (Alexander, 2010).

ARE WE SO DIFFERENT?

Just refer to your high school biology textbook for proof. You'll find that as members of the human race, we all are virtually the same on the inside. Research reveals that the majority of our differences are only skin deep. RACE: Are We So Different?, a science exhibit, confronts this much discussed topic. Developed by the American Anthropological Association, "the exhibit challenges visitors to examine the long-held notion that a certain number of 'races' exist within the human species and takes an in-depth look at the continuum of humankind, analyzing whether or not classifying people by race is a substantive measure." (www.understandingrace.org). The exhibition delves into science and historical contexts, as well as the social and cultural significance of the idea of race and racism. "It scrutinizes the misconceptions, confusion and other interpretations of the theory of race and the powerful social doctrines that have accompanied it."(www.understandingrace.org)

"Science has demonstrated that humans cannot be divided into 'races' based on physical attributes or genes," says John Mackay, former president and CEO of Discovery Place in Charlotte, N.C., which hosted the exhibit in 2010. "It's about the effects of geography and where people live … and how they interact with one another." (www.understandingrace.org).

On a genetic level, we are 99.9 percent similar. Why does the 0.01 percent (1/100 of 1 percent) account for a significant amount of how we view each other? That small percentage is often where we focus most of our attention. This needs to change if we're ever going to benefit from the talents and ideas from those around us (Taylor, 2006). Clotaire Rapaille, author of *The Culture Code*, says that the culture code is the unconscious meaning we apply to any given thing, including how we develop relationships. Most people do not realize that these differences can lead to how we process the same information in different ways, leaving long-lasting imprints. Experiences and how we feel about them create imprints that condition our thoughts and actions (Rapaille, 2006). These imprints influence us on an unconscious level. We do the majority of our learning by age 7. As a result, these imprint—which can result in stereotypes and myths—are difficult to change.

Research on the brain connection and biases, stereotypes, and prejudices reveals that our brains may be hardwired with these tendencies: We are born to judge. The brain may act on preconceptions we may not even realize we have. The brain structure that impacts biases, stereotypes, and judgments is the amygdala. To successfully manage the amygdala, we must develop the ability to control the daily emotional reactions it activates to everyday occurrences (Sherwood, 2009; Voss, 2013). This primitive control center, which was originally designed to keep us safe, automatically perceives others as threats. In addition to this barrier, John Dovido, a psychology professor at Yale University, says that as we are bombarded with repeated exposure to social stereotypes about various cultural groups, these associations become automatic. Furthermore, these quick judgments are made with little or no time to consciously prepare or make choices, and the results can be disturbing. For example: all Muslims are terrorists; overweight African Americans are lazy; elderly people are ineffectual.

Fortunately, the brain has another mechanism to help us: the neocortex. This part of the brain allows us to filter what we see and hear, and translate it into socially appropriate responses. How do you move beyond acknowledging people of color as one group? First, recognize this tendency exists.

Social neuroscientists believe that although it may be difficult to completely remove all biases, stereotypes, and misperceptions, these impulses, attitudes, and beliefs can be reshaped, which is the purpose of this book. Go to www.implicit.harvard.edu and take an online test in more than 90 subject areas to assess your knowledge of ethnicity, politics, and gender (Voss, 2013).

"UNCONSCIOUS BIAS"

"Unconscious Bias" is universal. They are mental short cuts based on social norms and stereotypes. In essence "unconscious bias" are prejudices we have but are unaware of them. This bias can be based on skin color, gender, age, height, weight, introvert/extrovert, disability, accent or names. (Guynn, 2015; Wilkie, 2014).

Unconscious bias is rooted in the brain in an area of the brain called the amygdala. The amygdala is associated with the temporal and frontal lobes. The temporal lobe stores information, social stereotypes, about people and objects. The frontal lobe is where we form impressions of others, empathy and reasoning. (Henneman, 2014). This has been used for survival so the brain can make quick decisions for safety or appropriateness. However, this survival mechanism does make it far more difficult to eliminate or minimize bias.

Scientist estimate we are exposed to as many as 11 million pieces of information at any time but our brains can only functionally deal with 40 pieces at one time. We therefore use a perceptual lens that filters out certain things and lets others in. As a result of these pre-established filters, we see things, and interpret them differently than other people might or we may not see them at all. In some cases our interpretations maybe so off that we have to examine how we know what is real, fact or fiction? This creates hundreds of seemingly irrational circumstances everyday that we must muddle through (Vozza, 2015).

So what is the impact? Unconscious bias causes us to make decisions in favor of our group or preferences to the detriment of other (Ross, 2008). We all have some type of prejudices and studies confirm that people harbor bias even when they explicitly believe that prejudice and discrimination are wrong (Henneman, 2014). Furthermore, gender stereo types can create several issues for women, people of color or transgendered, gay or bisexual individuals. As a result these groups may be left behind or limited in accessing leadership positions or receive unfavorable options no matter what they do, say or how they behave. For example there are extreme perceptions like women like they are too soft or too tough but never just right.

Danger detectors include thigs like decisions being made solely based on emotion. Many decisions are made emotionally and we collect facts to justify them. Oftentimes we launch in to this subconscious action before we even start thinking. In addition this good/bad person-the belief that good people are not biased and bad people are biased (Sullivan, 2015). Unconscious perceptions govern many of the important decisions or choices we make and have a profound effect on the lives of people in many ways. Understanding how unconscious bias affects how we value other is a major step in recognizing how differences can be viewed in the wrong ways. Here are several ways to begin to combat hidden bias:

1. Understand we all are biased;
2. Recognize as human being we make mistakes in our judgement;
3. Participate in training in a safe space to identify, uncover and discuss bias in your group or organization;
4. Examine your group or organizational culture for unconscious behaviors;
5. Know that we will never be free of all bias

REFERENCES

Catalyst (n.d.). *Double bind for women in leadership-Stereotype calculator*. Retrieved from http://www.catalyst.org/knowledge/double-bind-dilemma-women-leadership-damned-if-youdo-doomed-if-you-don't-0.

Cook, R. & Ross, H (2008). *Proven strategies for to address unconscious bias*. Retrieved from http://www.cookroos.comdocs/unconscoiusbias.pdf104

Guynn J. (05 May 2015). The growing business of detecting unconscious bias. Fast Company. Retrieved from http://www.usatoday.com/story/tech/2015/05/12/google-unconscious-bias-diversity/27055485/.

Hennermann, T. (09 February 2014). You biased? No it's your brain. Workforce. Retrieved from http://www.workforce.com/articles/20242-you-biased-no-its=your-brain.

Ross, H, J. (2010). *"Every day bias: Identifying and navigating unconscious judgement in our daily lives."* New York: Rowman & Littlefield Press.

Sullivan, S. (2014). *Good white people: The problem with middle class white anti-racism*. New York: SUMY Press.

Vozza, S. (16 April 2015). 5 common unconscious biases that lead to bad decisions. Fast Company. Retrieved from http://www.fastcompany.com/3045035/work-smart/5-common-unconscious-biases-that-lead-to-bad-decisions.

Wilkie, D. (01 December 2014). Rooting out hidden bias> SHRM. Retrieved from. http://.www.shrm.org/publications/hrmmagazinc/2014/1214/paes/1214-hidden-bias.aspx.

"What really matters is what happens in us, not to us."
—*ANONYMOUS*

"We are more alike than unalike"
—*MAYA ANGELOU*

MY THOUGHTS AND OBSERVATIONS

_____

_____

_____

_____

_____

_____

_____

_____

_____

_____

CHAPTER 3

WE'RE ALL A LITTLE WEIRD

. . . .

"We could learn a lot from crayons; some are sharp, some are pretty, some are dull, others bright; some have weird names, but they all have learned to live together in the same box."

—ROBERT FULGHUM,
ALL I REALLY NEED TO KNOW I LEARNED IN KINDERGARTEN

ARE YOU A LITTLE WEIRD?

Merriam-Webster defines *weird* as being "of strange or extraordinary character" (n.d.). Synonyms associated with the word "weird" are "odd," "eccentric," and "uncanny." But when you think about it, these words could apply to anyone.

John Ortberg, author of *Everybody's Normal Till You Get to Know Them*, agrees. "We all have flaws," he writes, "and we want to believe the illusion that all people are normal, so in developing relationships we do not always want to see the truth, which is we're all human beings that come with *as is* tags" (2003, p. 30). Ortberg suggests that you should appreciate your true self and allow others to really get to know you. Otherwise, you'll never enjoy the value of authentic relationships.

The idea of allowing others to see your true self is important because your failure to do so may be at the root of why you avoid developing relationships with people who are different. It's more comforting to speak and associate with people who are just like you: You already know the language, norms, and unspoken rules of that community. In other words, you fit in.

Angel is a perfect example. Her family moved to the United States from the Philippines when Angel was 8 years old. At that time, she spoke very little English. To Angel's embarrassment, her Filipino accent made her the center of teasing by neighborhood kids and classmates. To them, Angel spoke "funny." As a result, Angel refused to speak Filipino altogether and worked hard to refine her English. Not surprisingly, Angel learned and mastered English quickly, with barely a trace of an accent.

Before Angel knew it, she was entering college and claiming her place as a young adult. When she entered the University of North Carolina at Chapel Hill, Angel was impressed by the vibrant Asian American student groups on campus. To her surprise, many of Angel's Filipino classmates not only spoke fluent English, they had also retained their native tongue. For a brief time, Angel felt a hint of regret. She couldn't believe that the accent that had caused her so much grief as a child was cherished in this environment. Now, she longed to reclaim the culture she'd discarded so many years ago.

While she couldn't do anything about her past, Angel could design her future. She registered for Filipino classes to relearn the language she now loved and appreciated but could not speak. In addition, when Angel returned to her home in Charlotte, she explored activities she could participate in through the Carolinas Asian-American Chamber of Commerce to further her knowledge of Asian culture. The Asian Festival and the Charlotte Dragon Boat Festival—both of which brought people from Cambodia, China, Indonesia, Vietnam, and Malaysia together to celebrate their combined Asian heritage—were the highlights of the year. These were also activities that people of all cultures participated in and enjoyed, bridging the gap of old and new for Angel.

Thus, Angel came full circle. She went from immersing herself in her adopted culture, not wanting to appear weird, to accepting her differences so she could fit into the culture she had left behind. It's up to each of us to appreciate those qualities that are unique in others as we embrace them in ourselves. It's our weirdness that makes us all different—and human—and sometimes makes us shine. Our primary objective in building any relationship is to allow other people to get to know us in all of our weirdness, while we try to understand *and* accept them in all of theirs. Are you in agreement that we're all a little weird? If not, let's see if you fit into the *normal* category—and whether that is a good thing.

WHAT IS NORMAL?

Normal, or "the norm," is when an individual or group conforms to a certain type, standard, accepted rule, or common or natural condition. Michelle Johnson, author of *The Diversity Code*, describes it this way: "If we were to break it down and examine White People and People of Color and look at their experiences, no type of people share the exact same makeup. At some point, religion or spiritual worldview, age, region, upbringing, social-economic status, sexual orientation, physical abilities and disabilities, education and hobbies will cause divergence in perspective" (2011, p. 29-30).

People often attach themselves to norms when they want to be included, but norms themselves often perpetuate the fallacy that there is a norm and that those falling outside of certain parameters aren't *normal* (Johnson, 2011). If you're like the majority of people on the planet, you don't want to appear weird or not normal, so you go to great lengths to fit in—or at least feel as if you do. So the pressure to appear normal, though meant to help you enjoy your best life, can be the very thing that prevents you from truly appreciating the distinct characteristics in yourself and others—which is exactly what happened to Angel.

As you attempt to develop relationships with people who are different, remember that the concept of being normal is relative to the person who is making the assessment and the group to which he or she belongs. What's normal to a group of African American male medical students may be totally different from a group of White housewives. If you're serious about developing extraordinary relationships, it's up to you to be yourself and assess how you perceive others as well.

JUST LIKE US

During my first year in graduate school, I received a research assistantship, which gave me the opportunity to work with one of the faculty in my area of focus. In that role, I also became familiar with the inner operations of the department, which included working with the office staff and the administrative assistant. I spent a lot of time interacting with these individuals, and we got to know each other very well.

One day as I was copying materials, the administrative assistant remarked: "We are very fortunate to have you in the department. You are dependable and you are able to help us cover the office like the other RA's. I wish we could find more people like you. You are just like us."

I replayed her use of the phrases "I wish we could find more people like you" and "You are just like us." I assumed there was a compliment buried somewhere in her comments, but I wasn't sure what she meant. So I asked her to explain it to me.

"People like you," she responded. "I wish we could get more people like you."

I still did not understand her comments, but I did not pressure her for an explanation. It was not until a couple of days later that the meaning of her words came to me. From her perspective, I acted like the others in the department, and not like an African American. I was "normal," and I fit in. She wanted more RAs like me—African Americans who could blend into an environment that she and her colleagues considered normal. But the assimilation she perceived as a benefit was in reality a limitation that prevented both of us from building a relationship of any substance.

PUT ON A DIFFERENT PAIR OF GLASSES

Is developing extraordinary relationships as simple as putting on a different pair of glasses? Absolutely! You should make every effort to see things through someone else's eyes. This is key to changing the composition of the jellybeans in your cup. Your self-esteem can either paralyze you or motivate you to step into the unknown by reaching out to those who are not like you. Understanding your own strengths and weaknesses can impact your personal behavior and enable you to recognize and explore the differences in people.

Maslow's hierarchy of needs is a theory that examines how the relationships we develop are largely based on how adept we are at meeting our various needs. For instance, our lowest-level needs are physiological and pertain to survival: air, water, food, and shelter. As you would imagine, people with these needs are largely trying to connect with others who can help them master them. As you move higher up the hierarchy, relationships focus on success and autonomy, as individuals at these stages have the capacity to explore relationships in which they can examine themselves and the impact of others in their environment.

Maslow believed that everyone has the capacity to be involved in relationships in which differences are not just the focus but are integral to developing the capacity to be great. Excellence becomes a habit—not merely something we do at the right event, situation, or organization, or with the right people—and we are at our best when we allow ourselves to experience each other.

CREATIVITY AT WORK

If Mike DeLazzer's name does not immediately ring a bell, his creation will because it revolutionized an industry. Who hasn't heard of Redbox?

DeLazzer's story is one of frustration and being different, but it is also one about a rare individual with the capacity to see problems and find solutions. During a February 2014 interview, DeLazzer told me that growing up he did not seek approval or confirmation from his family or his peers. This "I don't care attitude" helped him develop persistence in pursing business opportunities later in life and motivated him to create innovative products when everyone told him they were impossible. As an entrepreneur, DeLazzer had the freedom to try many different things.

The invention of Redbox came out of his standing in a ridiculously long line one evening to rent a video at Blockbuster. He recalled asking himself, *Why is this line so long?* He then yelled, "Help! I am trapped in a Blockbuster" to the store attendant, but got no response. As he stood in line, DeLazzer recalled saying, "I am to going to find a solution and put Blockbuster out of business."

The solution came to him in an airport, where DeLazzer saw an "in motion" DVD retail kiosk with lots of staff but very few DVDs or customers. He then used that idea to develop software and an automated system for dispensing DVDs, Blu-Ray discs and video games via a kiosk known as a Redbox. In 2013 DeLazzer did exactly as he said he would: The company effectively put Blockbuster out of business. The billion-dollar company DeLazzer cofounded now has 42,000 kiosks in more than 34,000 locations.

Creativity is a core element in any discipline or industry, and according to Tom Kelley and David Kelly in the article "Reclaim Your Creative Confidence", it has impacted the rise and continued success we see in academia and business. The men believe everyone possesses unlimited creativity, but we must continue to rediscover it. Central to this creative process is the ability to open ourselves to the possibilities of what others have to offer—people who are different from you, outside of your comfort zone (Kelley & Kelley, 2012; Independent Youth Entrepreneur Conference, 2014, UNC-Charlotte; M. DeLazzer, Interview, February 28, 2014).

In the absence of the rules and regulations that govern society, the right brain is free to think intuitively outside the box to explore possibilities. The right brain allows us to identify similarities and empathize with others' experiences (Taylor, 2006). Daniel Pink (2005), author of *A Whole New Mind: Why Right Brainers Will Rule the Future*, asserts that we are in a "conceptual age" and says that by tapping into your right-brained abilities you will be more effective in your career and developing relationships. In particular, skills such as big-picture thinking, creativity, and empathy will be in high demand in the workplace.

EXPERIENCING OTHERS

Experiencing others means you have to move beyond your comfort level. As a speaker, I welcome opportunities to share what I have learned with others, and I was once asked to give a keynote address on creating a balanced life. Before I learned the details, I accepted the request. When I met with Roberta, the group's organizer, she explained that I was to speak to the volunteer group Hadassah, the Women's Zionist Organization of America. Hadassah, the Hebrew name of the biblical heroine Esther, was founded in 1912. With some 270,000 members, Hadassah is now one of the largest Jewish organizations in the world.

Roberta and I discussed my background and some of the key points she wanted me to share. A couple of weeks later, I arrived at the meeting site. I was nervous and experienced the initial anxiety most people have in unfamiliar surroundings. I was in a library conference room waiting to make a presentation to a room full of strangers. For a moment I felt as if I were having an out-of-body experience. I was pulled back into reality when I heard one of the group leaders sharing my bio and making an introduction.

Here I was: an African American, Christian woman speaking to a group of Jewish women I had never met. But, I soon realized that we had more in common than I at first thought. As I began to talk about how we as women take care of our families, our homes, and ourselves at the same time most of us work, our shared values became apparent. The lively discussion we engaged in afterward made our supposed differences vanish. I stay in touch with the women of Hadassah, who continue to invite me to their monthly luncheons and birthday celebrations.

So, if your fear of being a little weird or different is keeping you from connecting to someone, knowing that you are both afraid, how do you make the first move? Cautiously! Negotiating contact with people different from you can be a very real challenge. But it's an obstacle you *can* overcome and it's a step worth taking if you want more fulfilling relationships.

"Every one of us pretends to be healthier, kinder, smarter than we really are!"
JOHN ORTBERG

MY THOUGHTS AND OBSERVATIONS

_____

_____

_____

_____

_____

_____

_____

_____

_____

_____

_____

_____

_____

CHAPTER 4

DARE TO BE DIFFERENT

- -

"We don't attract what we want, but what we are.
Only by changing your thoughts will you change your life."

— JAMES ALLEN, BRITISH PHILOSOPHER

There's nothing wrong with observing that people look, speak, and act differently based on the values and experiences they bring to the table. Rather than being barriers to constructive communication, however, these differences should provide endless opportunities to better understand the people around you.

In what ways are people different? Believe it or not, the biggest differences are not biological—as in intelligence, mannerisms, or eye color—but rather those based on culture, perceptions, and stereotypes.

Culture is a complex concept that abounds with confusion, but simply put, *culture* refers to a group or community with which we share common experiences that shape our view of the world. It includes groups we are either born into, such as race, class, religion, or national origin, or those we join as we become aware of a shared history or common connections.

Stereotypes are sweeping generalizations formulated around every race and ethnicity, and, in general, are simple truths about a few individuals that are applied, often incorrectly, to an entire group of people. Stereotypes can be based on characteristics, traits, or roles. People often rely on stereotypes for clues about how they should interact with a specific group or respond in a particular setting. Stereotypes can be positive—all Blacks are great dancers, for example—but they can still negatively impact the referenced group and ultimately lead to discrimination.

While stereotyping in all its forms can be hurtful and oppressive, taken in a lighter vein, stereotypes can be a source of parody and humor. Consider such classic movies as *Airplane!* or *Blazing Saddles*. One of the foundations for developing extraordinary relationships is the ability to understand someone else's feelings, thoughts, and motives. Understanding these important elements opens the door for you to begin to know how your own feelings and thoughts impact others.

Stereotypes can also lead to prejudice and impact developing empathy. Prejudice—which is more about prejudging others without having adequate information, using past experiences or the opinions of others to make assumptions—is a socially endorsed way of life, so when you mix the two together, individuals can have a difficult time distinguishing appropriate from offensive behavior.

As you try to connect with people, it's important that you also examine these false beliefs. Political correctness aside, there are many colorful (no pun intended) assumptions about people in relation to their racial backgrounds. Many stereotypes come from natural tendencies that, in the short term, help people make sense of a complicated world. In the long term, however, these same tendencies further complicate that world. The recognition of prejudices, biases, and stereotypes that you do not understand is the prerequisite for undoing your false ideas.

FACTS, FICTION AND MYTHS

Following are 20 common statements often associated with various groups of people. Review the list and honestly assess the statements based on your own views and values to be facts, fiction, or myths:

	Fact	Fiction	Myth
1. White men in the workforce are always in charge.	O	O	O
2. Gen Xers are slackers at work and job-hop to get ahead.	O	O	O
3. Africa is a primitive, wild, poor, and underdeveloped continent.	O	O	O
4. All Latinos speak Spanish.	O	O	O
5. All Christians are homophobic.	O	O	O
6. Women are bad drivers.	O	O	O
7. African Americans love watermelon.	O	O	O
8. All Asians are smart.	O	O	O
9. African Americans are lazy.	O	O	O
10. Too many Hispanics live in one house.	O	O	O
11. People who speak with an accent are less intelligent.	O	O	O
12. Women are blabbermouths.	O	O	O
13. "Latino" and "Hispanic" have the same meaning.	O	O	O
14. All illegal immigrants to the United States are from Mexico.	O	O	O
15. All Arabs are Muslims.	O	O	O
16. Traditionalists cannot learn technology.	O	O	O
17. Millennials have a strong sense of civic duty.	O	O	O
18. Native Americans love gambling.	O	O	O
19. Baby Boomers are workaholics.	O	O	O
20. All Asians are alike.	O	O	O

As you evaluated these statements, were you able to distinguish fact from myth or fiction?

Myths in our society are so strong that even in the face of verified research to the contrary, people often take them into consideration when developing relationships.

Your responses may not have been as straightforward as you thought they might be, because many of these assumptions have been passed down for generations. Sometimes you've believed something for so long, it feels like fact. Other times the truth has been stretched so far it becomes a lie.

The question is: Which of these statements are true today? Let's take a closer look.

1. White men in the work force are always in charge. Although the corporate world is primarily dominated by white men, women and other minorities continue to climb the career ladder. According to an August 2015 study released by CreditDonkey®, women hold 4.8 percent of CEO positions at Fortune 500 companies. Xerox's Ursula Burns is the only African American among them. African Americans represent approximately 1 percent of Fortune 500 CEOs. Twenty-three Fortune 500 CEOs, or 4 percent, are considered minorities, which include African Americans, Asians, and Latin Americans.

Recent statistics from Pew Research show that women are increasingly taking jobs in managerial positions. In 2013, 52.2 percent of managerial and professional occupations were held by women, up from 30.6 percent in 1968. Even so, according to a survey of top leaders from midmarket businesses throughout the United States, in 2014 only 22 percent of senior managers were women.

2. Gen Xers are slackers at work and job-hop to get ahead. The post–Baby Boomer group acquired this dubious distinction because of a perceived lack of work ethic (in at 8:00 a.m., out by 5:00 p.m.), but that's only part of the story. Gen Xers value a work–life balance because they have learned through experience that jobs can be eliminated with little warning. Rather than rely on institutions for long-term security, they invest in their own development, such as through entrepreneurial pursuits. In the workplace, Gen Xers value autonomy coupled with responsibility and they want flexible hours in an informal work environment—with little supervision.

3. Africa is a primitive, wild, poor, and underdeveloped continent. Africa is the second-largest continent on the planet, accounting for 20 percent of the landmass in the world. With more than 800 million people living in 54 countries, it represents one-seventh of the earth's population. Although natural resources are abundant, Africa remains the world's poorest and most underdeveloped continent. Causes include political corruption, human rights violations, illiteracy, lack of access to foreign capital, and tribal and military conflict, which range from genocide to guerilla warfare.

The wealthiest country in Africa is Namibia, where production of minerals, including diamonds, generates a GDP of more than $16 billion. However, one-half of the country lives below the poverty line. The Democratic Republic of the Congo is the poorest country in Africa, with a GDP per capita of $394.25.

4. All Latinos speak Spanish. Latin American countries are those with a Latin-derived national language. Of the 400 million people who speak Castilian Spanish, 300 million live in Latin American nations. Spanish is the official language of all Latin American countries—with the exception of Brazil, where Portuguese is the national language. In addition to Portuguese, Japanese is spoken by more than 2 million people. A combination of Spanish, Japanese, and Mandarin is spoken in Peru, which has large populations of Chinese and Japanese.

The number of Spanish speakers in the United States is projected to grow to approximately 40 million people by 2020, but this increase, surprisingly, is within non-Hispanic and non-Latino populations. According to Mark Hugo Lopez of the Pew Research Center, "Even though the number of Spanish speakers is projected to grow, among Latinos and Hispanics, the share that speak Spanish is projected to fall from 75 percent to 66 percent." The decrease is due to the stigma associated with the language, as well as the third-generation Latino and Hispanic populations, who are more likely than immigrant groups to be English dominant. (http://www.pewhispanic.org/2013/07/23/a-growing-share-of-latinos-get-their-news-in-english/; Pp. 1-4).

5. All Christians are homophobic. By definition, homophobia is fear of gay people, but its meaning has been broadened to include hate for gay people. While the Bible strongly condemns homosexuality, it never instructs gay people to be hated.

The truth is that homophobia is not confined to any one segment of society: Both Christians and non-Christians can be homophobic—and certainly not all Christians are homophobic. Being yourself and not being judged is at the core of valuing differences, but the debate on homosexuality within the Christian community will continue despite great strides that have been made in the gay and lesbian communities in recent years. Most people have learned to look beyond sexuality and understand and accept gay people as contributing members to our diverse society.

6. Women are bad drivers. Insurance firms regularly confirm that male drivers have the most accidents. They also report that, in general, women are more cautious drivers and are less likely to speed or drive under the influence of alcohol or drugs, when compared to men. In fact, young men have the greatest numbers of automobile accidents.

7. African Americans love watermelon. Though statistics aren't necessary to convey the ridiculousness of the watermelon stereotype, data reveals that African Americans actually eat less watermelon than others. The Department of Agriculture reports that White people eat more watermelon than their Black counterparts, but the largest consumers of watermelon per capita are Asians and Hispanics.

8. All Asians are smart. Statistical data on achievement does support that Asian Americans and Asian populations around the world continue to outperform American students. Simultaneously, numerous Asian students who require academic assistance often fall through the cracks, because it is assumed that all Asians are intelligent and do not need tutoring.

A 2008 article published in *Diverse Issues in Higher Education* stated that Asian American students, due to high expectations and parental and peer pressure, were more likely than Caucasian students to report difficulties with stress, sleep, and feelings of hopelessness—yet they were less likely to seek counseling. Cornell University found that Asian American college students were more likely to seek medical leave, more likely to go on academic probation, and less likely to graduate in four years than their peers. The Coalition for Asian American Children and Families discovered that 33 percent of Asian American students drop out of high school or don't graduate on time, perhaps because 11.8 percent of Asian Americans live below the poverty line.

9. African Americans are lazy. This myth and stereotype began during the slave trade, which is ironic, because if you examine the work life of slaves, you'll find that being lazy was not an option. Louisiana physician Samuel A. Cartwright's 1851 "Report on the Diseases and Physical Peculiarities of the Negro Race" set the stage for this stereotype. Cartwright believed there were specific disorders that affected African American slaves, one of them being dysaethesia aethiopica. The symptoms included a refusal to work, disobedience, and insolence. This disorder was the basis for the belief that slaves needed constant supervision to complete their work.

The perception of African American laziness continued with 20th- and 21st-century beliefs about work ethic and welfare assistance. African Americans have been singled out as the only U.S. demographic that is dependent on government programs such as food stamps, temporary assistance for needy families, and Supplemental Security Income, which as a whole are defined as welfare. However, the following 2014 statistics provided by the U.S. Department of Health and Human Services and the U.S. Department of Commerce indicate:

- Total U.S. population: 314 million.
- Total number of Americans on welfare: 12,800,000.
- Total U.S. population on welfare: 4.1 percent.
- Percentage of White recipients of welfare: 38.8 percent.
- Percentage of Black recipients of welfare: 39.8 percent.
- Percentage of Hispanic/Latino recipients of welfare: 15.7 percent.
- Percentage of Asian recipients of welfare 2.4 percent.
- Percentage of "other" recipients of welfare: 3.3 percent.

When factoring these statistics, it is important to consider that Caucasians are 77 percent of the population, while African-Americans comprise 13.1 percent of the population.

10. Too many Hispanic/Latino Americans live in one house. Extended family is a cornerstone of the Hispanic/Latino culture. Grandparents, parents, and children often live under the same roof, placing the needs of the family ahead of individual concerns. Generally speaking, Hispanic/Latino American children and adolescents learn to show respect for authority, the patriarchal family structure, and extended family members.

11. People with accents are less intelligent. Everyone speaks with some sort of accent, defined by sociolinguistics as a manner of pronunciation peculiar to a particular individual, location, or nation—and accents play crucial roles in how we judge people. Often confused with dialect (linguistic differences), accents focus on the voice, pronunciation, and the distinction of vowels and consonants.

Accents can identify an individual's geographic location—in the region of a country or in the world. Accents can also identify socioeconomic or social status. Elite status and intelligence have often been associated with a British accent. An informal study several years ago concluded that parents preferred British nannies to American nannies because they sounded more intelligent.

Accents can also carry negative stereotypes. People of color (African Americans, Latinos, and Hispanics), especially those born in an inner city, where Ebonics is accepted; or in the Low Country of South Carolina, where Gullah is spoken; or even New Orleans, where Creole colorfully rings, may be judged as less educated or less intelligent because they do not use standard English. Even Whites born in the South are often ridiculed by their Northern peers.

Accents are initial points of analyses—and because they are often the first things noticed about a person, they can either interfere with or encourage relationship development. Distinct foreign or ethnic-based accents can even be obstacles during the employment and educational process.

In an article that appeared in the December 10, 2010, issue of *Science Daily*, Tamara Rakic says that accents may have more influence on how we judge people than appearance. Accents and language quickly categorize people by temperament, age, state of mind, and ethnic background.

12. Women are blabbermouths. Let's just say that women are big talkers, especially when compared to their male counterparts, and science agrees. The areas in the brain that manage language are more than 17 percent larger in women than men. Women are also big multitaskers and can process language in both hemispheres, while men generally stick to the dominant side of their brains. There's more: Women can transfer data much more quickly than men from one side of the brain to the other due to a larger corpus callosum, a thick band of nerve fibers that divides the brain into hemispheres.

According to communications expert Deborah Tannen, men, on average, use more words than women. However, taking into account the situation, the reason for speaking, the person to whom you are speaking, and the manner in which words are used reveals more about speaking patterns. In addition, cultural and gender difference must be understood. Gender distinctions are built into who we talk to and how we talk to them. These differences shouldn't be viewed as a deficit, but rather as a basis for clearer communication.

Tannen says that women engage in "rapport talk" and men in "reporting talk." Women use rapport talk to develop connections and intimacy, and tend to speak more in private/small group settings. As a result, women focus on discovering similarities and developing relationships. Men use reporting talk for information, to maintain control, and to protect themselves in conversations. They prefer speaking in public and in large settings in which they are the center of attention and can speak as much as possible to be recognized and acknowledged.

13. "Latino" and "Hispanic" mean the same thing. While the two terms are sometimes used interchangeably, Hispanic is a narrower term, generally referring to persons of Spanish-speaking origin or ancestry. Latino is more frequently used to refer to those of Latin American origin or ancestry.

14. All illegal immigrants to the United States are Mexicans. The Pew Hispanic Research Center found that illegal immigration from Mexico has actually declined in recent years. In 2007 an estimated 7 million unauthorized immigrants lived in the United States. Three years later, that number had dropped to 6.5 million. As of 2010 Mexicans comprised 58 percent of undocumented immigrants living in the United States. Unauthorized migrants from elsewhere in Latin America made up 23 percent of the unauthorized population, followed by those from Asia (11 percent), Europe and Canada (4 percent), and Africa (3 percent).

15. All Arabs are Muslims. Although the term "Arab" originally referred to the people who inhabited the northern and central portions of the Arabian Peninsula, today the word has come to represent those who speak the Arabic language. While most Arabs practice Islam, Christianity and Judaism are also practiced. Islam is not an Arabic religion; Muslims are found throughout the world.

16. Traditionalists cannot learn technology. Born between the years 1922 and 1943, this generation has witnessed the most dramatic shifts in society as the world has moved from industrialism to the technology age. Because traditionalists are over age 70, it is assumed that intellectually they do not have the capacity to manage technological devices such as computers, laptops, and mobile devices—or social media.

The truth is that although they may prefer face-to-face or written communication, there is no cognitive evidence to support this statement. However, the digital divide exists in terms of how fast technology evolves. It will be interesting to see how this generation stays abreast of constantly changing updates.

17. Millennials have a strong sense of civic duty. Although this generation has a stigma of being self-centered and caring more about pop culture than their friends and families, Millennials take pride in volunteer work and using the power of the Internet and social media to develop and participate in activism and politics.

18. Native Americans love gambling. Although many people believe that money from casinos has supplied Native Americans with more than enough financial resources, of the 560 Indian nations, only 224 are involved in the gaming industry. Of those 224, only a few earn enough revenue to support their tribes.

Large-scale gaming did not emerge until the 1980s, when the Indian Gaming Regulatory Act formally recognized the rights of Native Americans to conduct gaming operations. Since that time, gaming has become a means for Native American tribes to provide sources of employment, replenish impoverished communities, and preserve their culture. Native Americans don't love gambling; they simply appreciate the opportunities it provides.

19. Baby Boomers are workaholics. As the largest population in the workforce, Baby Boomers have a strong work ethic and are committed to long hours, as well as to climbing the ladder of corporate success. While moving to the next level has always been important, the most stressed generation in the American workforce struggles to find a work–life balance. Many want to simplify their lives; while others—even in retirement—are building second careers.

20. All Asians are alike. This one-dimensional perspective does not take into account the diversity within ethnic groups. The global Asian population is composed of natives of Korea, China, Japan, Malaysia, Vietnam, and many other countries, each with its own distinct culture—and facial features. (See how proficient you are in identifying Asian groups by taking the test: www.AllLookSame.com; Reyes-Chow, 2012).

Are you surprised that so few of the above statements are factual? As you can see, a truth can easily be transformed into a lie when misinterpreted, resulting in misunderstandings about a cultural group member's thoughts, feelings, or motives.

While generalizations about people, cultures, situations, geographical locations, and philosophies can highlight similarities, more often they obscure differences in unintended ways. Simple categories cannot capture an individual's unique qualities.

To combat the tendency to stereotype people, make a list of clichés you have about a particular group. Then consider how these beliefs have affected your interaction (or lack thereof) with that group. Finally, determine if there is any truth to your belief. If there is, uncover ways that you can develop relationships with the people in that group and move beyond your limitations.

"I am invisible; understand, simply because people refuse to see me."
—*RALPH ELLISON, AUTHOR OF* THE INVISIBLE MAN

MY THOUGHTS AND OBSERVATIONS

_____

_____

_____

_____

_____

_____

_____

_____

_____

_____

_____

_____

CHAPTER 5

JUDGE NOT

• •

"If you judge people, you have no time to love them."

—*MOTHER TERESA*

We often think we're accepting of people, but in reality, we're constantly judging them based on our expectations. We view others through our own lenses and wonder why they're not measuring up. This chapter explores why we are unable to welcome differences or appreciate the uniqueness in others, and why we react the way we do when the truth is revealed.

ARE YOU THE JUDGE?

Several years ago, I attended a performance by Chanticleer, an international all-male a cappella group known for its orchestral voices. After I sat down and had an opportunity to study the audience, I realized that my guest and I were two of only four people of color in the roughly 950-member audience.

Following the concert, my friend and I were invited to a party the artists were attending. As we made our way through the crowd, we got "the look" from several of the guests. The party was perceived as a VIP event, and some of the guests seemed to question our presence. However, the host—a well-respected board member of the organization sponsoring the performance—greeted us with a smile.

As you might imagine, the attitudes of the other guests began to soften. I found it interesting that those who initially weren't interested in speaking to us wanted to know more about my friend and me after the host personally introduced us to others in the room. I'm not sure why some of the guests seemed to be uncomfortable with our presence. It could have been our age; we were much younger than most of the attendees. It could have been our skin color, or it simply could have been that we were new faces in the crowd. Whatever the case, the other guests were judging us without getting to know us. We've all been in situations like this—the judge and the judged—but at some point, we need to determine the reasons we make decisions about the people with whom we interact and build relationships. Why? It's the right thing to do.

SNAP JUDGMENTS

Are you familiar with heuristics? Heuristics are cognitive shortcuts used to make routine decisions and solve problems, allowing us to navigate our daily lives with ease. For example, it's 5 p.m. and you instinctively take back roads to pick up your child at daycare, avoiding rush-hour traffic. It's cloudy and you hear thunder, so you grab your umbrella. Your habits and experiences eliminate the need to think through every minor choice and detail of life.

While heuristics are meant to speed up problem-solving and decision-making processes, these same cues are potential relationship traps. In an effort to use familiarity and comfort to save time, heuristics can lead to inaccurate judgments about events, situations, and people.

You make decisions about how you develop relationships in the same manner you make other snap judgments. Based on first impressions, you select familiar-looking individuals who make you feel comfortable and reject those with whom you don't have an immediate connection. In the process, you often overlook more relevant information and risk turning a heuristic into an act of prejudice. Although heuristics are used to classify and categorize people, you can rein in hasty judgments if you recognize how you make decisions and change your course of action, if necessary (*U.S. News & World Report*, 2011).

Of utmost importance is finding balance. If you can gather more information before reaching a conclusion about someone, do so. Use caution, however. Overthinking to appraise an individual may have the opposite effect and prove to be an obstacle to meeting people who are different (Anthes, 2012; Pincott, 2012).

If you cannot move past initial judgments, you miss out on opportunities to share your own gifts, as well as enjoy someone else's contributions to this world. If you focus on your perception of an individual's current circumstances, you may never get to know who the person really is, or what he or she has the potential to become.

MOVING PAST YOUR FEARS

Uncertainty is difficult for the human mind to grasp; the mind actually prefers snap judgments. According to risk expert David Ropeik (2010), author of *How Risky Is It, Really? Why Our Fears Don't Always Match the Facts*, in many instances, you have to quickly decide if something is dangerous, which increases your chances of survival. Fear is the most ancient, efficient, and effective security system in the world. Your innate fears are survival mechanisms tucked into the amygdala, the emotional control center of the brain.

Fear is at the core of why we often jump to judge others, and insecurity is the root of many of our unfounded fears. Before you can overcome your fears, you need to think about why they exist. The ability to manage fear is important in channeling that energy into purposeful action that can assist you in developing relationships with people who are different. Review the following examples to determine if any of them sound like you:

- **Fear of the unknown:** Punam Singh is Indian. She has invited you to her home countless times for dinner. You continue to make polite excuses, but she's catching on that something is wrong. The truth is you're concerned about the menu. You're not sure that you'll like what she prepares, and you don't want to offend her. Food has significant importance in many cultures when it comes to building relationships, and you don't want to risk ruining your friendship.

- **Fear of loss:** Sue has been a member of Antioch Baptist Church for 40 years. Her children, grandchildren, and great-grandchildren have all been baptized at that church. Though the church has traditionally had an African American congregation, Sue notices that the racial composition is changing. At first, she is delighted to see different faces and welcomes the newcomers with open arms. But as she sees marked changes in the faces in the pulpit, the choir, the style of music, and the message, she is skeptical and concerned that she no longer fits in.

- **Fear of getting something you don't want:** Timothy was a diligent employee who had worked at the same company for 25 years. Then the company began to aggressively hire Gen Xers and Millennials to remain competitive in the marketplace. Timothy understands the need to attract and cultivate young talent, but the past couple of years, he has noticed that his colleagues are much younger than he. Timothy now feels insecure and worries about keeping up with the talent emerging in the organization.

- **Fear of revealing your true self:** James is Mr. Popularity at work and play. He enjoys being the corporate star from 9 a.m. to 5 p.m. and hanging with the gang after work. Most of the people he interacts with are White males. He is friendly to the coworkers who can further his career and understands that others view him in the same manner. But when the company hires a Chinese marketing executive, James doesn't have a clue as to how he should relate to him. Kim doesn't laugh at his jokes, is very serious about even the most mundane activities, and comes off as quite cold. James begins to wonder how he can get through to the guy since Kim is standing in the way of his next promotion.

- **Fear of consequences:** Several years ago Susan was introduced to Karen. The two seemed to have similar backgrounds. Both had Ph.Ds in education, were around the same age, had two children and shared a love for working with college students. The person who made the introduction believed the two young women would become fast friends. However, as Susan began to get to know Karen, she learned that there was much more to her than met the eye. Karen was an unemployed, homeless, single mother of two college-age children, with no relatives in town. Susan was afraid that if she continued the friendship with Karen, she'd become too involved with her problems.

- **Fear of isolation by affiliation:** I was recently at a holiday networking event that was designed to give people an opportunity to connect and reconnect with people in the organization. As I mingled, I came across some of my closest friends. While we were catching up, we noticed board member Elizabeth, whom I knew well, coming toward us. However, instead of speaking to us, Elizabeth whizzed past without acknowledging us at all. Though my friends were stunned and offended, I wasn't surprised. Elizabeth was known for associating with only those who could further her standing in the community. If she needed you, you'd get her undivided attention. If not, you'd get the brush-off. I did not want to reveal how close I was to Elizabeth because my other friends might have believed I was also opportunistic.

- **Fear of responsibility:** Marie was on the plane ready to hook up her Wi-Fi when the person sitting next to her started talking. Tara was a breath of fresh air—funny and a great conversationalist. Like Marie, Tara was a married mom dealing with the death of a parent. The two seemed destined to become friends. Though Marie was initially concerned about the four-hour plane ride, time flew by as she learned about Tara's various adventures and laughed at her jokes. When the plane landed, Marie wondered whether this would be a one-time meeting or a long-standing relationship. To Marie, a friendship would require phone calls, visits, and e-mails. She was hesitant to give her contact information to Tara or ask for hers because she did not want to feel obligated to stay in touch. Could she add developing a new friendship to her already full plate? (Kelley & Kelley, 2012)

FACING THE TRUTH

So, how do you overcome your fears? First, you have to acknowledge that those fears exist. Next, you must admit that you are judging others. I've had to do that myself a few times. In one of the first multicultural workshops I presented for a large corporate client, I was asked to develop an activity based on the phrase "we all have a little redneck in us." "Redneck" is a derogatory term that refers to uneducated Southern white farmers—rednecks because they worked outside and their necks were sunburned.

The term was popularized by comedian Jeff Foxworthy, who is known for his "you might be a redneck" one-liners. "You might be a redneck if you think the last words to the *Star Spangled Banner* are 'gentlemen start your engines,'" he quips.

More recently, in the blockbuster movie *The Blind Side*, rednecks were referenced, but in an unexpected situation. In one scene, Leigh Ann and Sean Tuohy's adopted African American son, Michael Oher, chooses a Ford Rotundra upon getting his driver's license. "You bought him a truck?" the Tuohys' daughter, Collins, asks her dad. "Yeah, Michael thinks he's a redneck," he replies.

Despite the current acceptance of the use of the word "redneck" in everyday language, I was reluctant to conduct activities based on this term because of my own stereotypes. As an African American woman, I associate rednecks with the Confederate flag, White extremism, and the KKK. Plus, I knew I would be delivering the material to an all-White, male audience of energy supervisors, technicians, engineers, and repairmen. Truth be told, I was nervous, but I also recognized that the activity could have relevance beyond this particular client.

So, we came up with the following activity: A lady takes her automobile to a mechanic, who happens to be a classic redneck, for repairs. The customer is skeptical at first about leaving her car, but decides to do so anyway. Upon her return she is greeted by the mechanic's smiling face and proud stance. Not only does he fix the car, he buffs out dents and scratches and takes care of other minor repairs. At the end of the exercise, we tell the audience that you can't judge a redneck by his cover to reveal how easy it is to judge others based on assumptions.

Fast forward to 2010, when I came face-to-face with my own "redneck moment." As I was leaving campus one afternoon, my car started to shake uncontrollably. I turned into the nearest shopping center, parked my car, and, upon inspection, saw that my tire was completely flat. As I contemplated my options, an air conditioning repair truck pulled into the parking space directly in front of my car. The two men inside got out and one asked, "Ma'am, do you need any help?" I politely but quickly answered, "No thank you. I am going to call AAA." He acknowledged my reply and went into Arby's for lunch. I then cleaned out the contents of my trunk to locate the spare tire and wait for AAA to arrive.

Thirty minutes later, I was still waiting. When the two men came outside, they got back in their truck, but didn't start it. Momentarily, there was a knock on my window. "Ma'am, can we help you?" one of them asked. "I am still waiting for AAA," I replied. He then assured me that he and his friend could have the tire changed in five minutes. I paused for a moment and asked myself, *Why am I not letting them help me? I am not in fear of my life.* I then got out of the car and showed them the spare tire. Just like he said, the two men changed the flat tire quickly. I thanked them several times, and, just as fast as they'd arrived, they were back in their truck and on their way.

Why did I initially refuse their help? Because I quickly judged these men based on their appearance. They were dressed in white T-shirts and dirty, saggy jeans, and they both had red necks from working in the sun. How many times do we refuse help, insight or even a kind gesture because of predetermined notions? If you had been one of these two men, would you have waited patiently for me to come around, knowing you had been judged? Patience is a virtue when developing extraordinary relationships. It often helps us move past our initial judgments and fears and allows us to get to know someone, if only for a fleeting moment.

THE FINAL VERDICT

We are all guilty of judging people, and we need to acknowledge when we do it and why. Noted author and leadership expert Ken Blanchard relates an experience dealing with differences he had as a young boy.

> "I was on the basketball team at my school, and we were going to play a rival team across town. There were Black players on the other team, and one in particular caught my attention. He was the tallest player on the team. He would easily make anyone who had to guard him uneasy. Although the other team won the game, I was able to talk to this tall guard for a few minutes afterward. He was the nicest guy, and as a kid I could not immediately see that because of his size. That day made me realize how important it is to not judge people before I get to know them" (Interview with Ken Blanchard, Chapel Hill, March 7, 2006).

Once you face the truth, you can move past stereotypes, biases, and assumptions so that you're able to experience humanity in its fullest. If you're ready to enjoy a higher level of diverse relationships, you can do that now by simply asking yourself a few simple questions about how you interact with others. Be willing to honestly assess your responses.

"Do not judge people before you have experienced their world."
— *JOYCE MEYER*

MY THOUGHTS AND OBSERVATIONS

_____

_____

_____

_____

_____

_____

_____

_____

_____

_____

_____

_____

_____

CHAPTER 6

CAN'T WE ALL JUST GET ALONG?

∙∙

"The truth will set you free. But first it will piss you off."

— *GLORIA STEINEM*

In March 2010 Gloria Steinem was a guest speaker for the Women's and Gender Studies program at the University of North Carolina in Charlotte. After a stirring presentation, Steinem sat down with me to discuss race and relationships in these changing times. The following is an edited version of the interview.

Dr. Felecia Harris: Why do you think we're still discussing racial issues in the new millennium?

Gloria Steinem: It's not that we're stuck on stupid; it's just that many of us are simply stuck. We're afraid that by getting to know people who are different, we will somehow lose a part of ourselves that we will never get back.

DFH: I'm currently working on a book about developing diverse relationships and how essential this is for a more fulfilling personal and professional life. Why do you think diverse relationship building is a challenge for so many of us?

GS: Logically, it doesn't make sense. On a planet as diverse as ours, you'd think we'd seize every opportunity we could to connect with the people that can best teach us about it. Instead, we put up fronts and facades so that others never really get to know us. At the same time, we never really get to know them.

DFH: So how do you think this challenge can be resolved?

GS: We need to dismantle the barriers we have put up that prevent us from truly revealing our discomfort so we can get to the truth. We allow fear to keep us from asking the questions we really want to know the most, and when we do attempt to ask about those things we're afraid to discuss, we only further complicate the situation because trust and respect were never fully developed. Not only do we not get an answer, but our inquiry creates a difficult barrier that will take more time to remove.

DFH: So are you saying our inability to relate will improve over time?

GS: It is precisely the lack of investment in time and thought that keeps many of us from truly developing diverse relationships. We all are a little egocentric. By nature, we bring the focus on ourselves in order to accept others. We are own worst enemies. We talk ourselves out of experiencing something new.

DFH: Do you think fear plays a role in why we're not connecting the way we should?

GS: The unknown is what we fear, but we all are remarkable human beings, and we can learn to respect those who are different from us by simply showing respect. Respecting their gender, the way they talk, dress, interact, and share information. Basic respect for the human spirit is what saves us.

Gandhi has this wonderful phrase: "One million acts of simple kindness can change a culture." Simply accepting and embracing differences is the hallmark of respect. Is this too simple? Remember, it only takes one person at a time, one moment at a time, and one day at a time for change.

DFH: So, you do believe change is possible?

GS: Fortunately, you are not just a product of your circumstances. So, if you didn't grow up around African American, Russian, Indian, Asian, Native American, Italian, French, or some other nationality, you must still be willing to tolerate a lot of ambiguity and be able to step back to think, reflect, and accept differences and change. It starts one person at a time.

"I freed thousands of slaves, and could have freed thousands more,
if they had known they were slaves."
—*HARRIET TUBMAN*

MY THOUGHTS AND OBSERVATIONS

_____

_____

_____

_____

_____

_____

_____

_____

_____

_____

_____

_____

CHAPTER 7

LOST IN TRANSLATION

• •

"We all struggle with our failure to communicate
and our failure to reach beyond fear to love people."

— *MIRA SORVINO*

Most of us know at least one person who can strike up a conversation anytime, anywhere, with anyone; yet, for every person who is well versed in the art of conversation, there are dozens of others who struggle with the simplest of exchanges. This chapter examines effective communication and explains why ineffective communication skills can inhibit the development of new relationships. Specific steps for improving your skills are explored so that you can make better connections with people who are different from you—and ultimately enjoy fulfilling relationships that go beyond skin deep.

The word "communication" is derived from the Latin root word *communis*, or common. That's no surprise because you have to establish common ground—at least momentarily—to effectively communicate with a person on any level. In fact, the listener is motivated to tune into your message because you've somehow convinced him or her that you have something in common—whether it is attitudes, ideas, or an understanding that elements of the conversation are relevant to him or her.

According to *Merriam-Webster*, *communication* is "the act or process of using words, sounds, signs or behaviors to express or exchange information, or to express ideas, thoughts, feelings, etc., to someone else" (n.d.). Essentially, the purpose of communication is to inform, entertain, and persuade. I'll add "inquire," because an essential element of communication is receiving information as well.

ACTIONS SPEAK LOUDER THAN WORDS

Communication is categorized as intentional or unintentional. Intentional communication is carried out with purpose and refers to the actual words used, whether in verbal or written form. Successful intentional communication occurs when three elements are present: 1) the receiver understands the message; 2) the message accomplishes its intended purpose; and 3) the sender and the recipient remain on favorable terms during the communications process.

Unintentional, or nonverbal, communication includes facial expressions, tone of voice, and body language. Communication experts estimate that nonverbal communication comprises as much as 90 percent of face-to-face interaction. One UCLA study indicates that effective communication is determined by: 7 percent words; 38 percent voice; and 55 percent nonverbal communication. In fact, nonverbal cues have more than four times the impact of verbal ones when the two are used in combination (Argyle, Salter, Nicholson, Williams, & Burgess, 1970; Rosenthal, Hall, DiMatteo, Rogers, & Archer, 1979).

Nonverbal cues are powerful and can reveal more than a person's spoken words. If a person says one thing but his nonverbal communication indicates another, pay attention to the nonverbal communication. Understanding these nonverbal messages can make all the difference in developing a new relationship (Heathfield, 2016).

MICROMESSAGING

Micromessaging is a universally understood language that we begin interpreting and utilizing at birth. Micromessages reveal much about our biases and preconceived notions and carry powerful clues as to what exists between the lines—the hidden assumptions based on race, gender, class, religion, and nationality. Although micro messages reveal our true feelings, they are also incomplete pictures and are therefore difficult to define (Young, 2007).

According to Stephen Young, author of *Micromessaging: Why Great Leadership Is Beyond Words*, "Micro messaging examines the nuanced behaviors that we all blindly use and react to in our dealings with others." Micromessages are universal in their application, yet all cultures have their own unique forms of sending and receiving these messages (2007, pp. 77, 87–89; 105). Even so, micromessages are influenced by our individual backgrounds and experiences.

When we develop relationships with people who are culturally different, we must understand that we cannot use our own perspectives to filter their messages. We must develop the ability to use multidimensional mirrors as a means to see our own behaviors and make adjustments when necessary. There is no set formula that works in all situations, but it is important to learn human dynamics and have an awareness of what and how we communicate (Young, 2007).

YOUR FACE SPEAKS A THOUSAND WORDS

Facial expressions are one of the most important nonverbal forms of micro messaging. Almost like a truth serum, facial expressions reveal concealed emotions and clues about what we are thinking even when verbal communication reads false. Faces also provide windows into the mechanisms that govern our emotional and social lives. As a result, the face is the site of multiple signals and messages. Some of these messages include:

- **Emotions:** happiness, sadness, anger, disgust, surprise, and fear
- **Emblems:** culturally specific symbolic communications, such as a wink or eye contact
- **Illustrators:** actions that accompany and highlight speech, such as a raised brow
- **Regulators:** nonverbal conversational mediators, such as nods or smiles

(Cacioppo, Hager, & Ekman, 2016; Ekman & Friesen, 1975; Ekman (2016)

Every part of your face communicates something. Facial expressions can change the messages you send and alter how you receive them. Since you usually do not see your own face, you are often unaware of its total impact. Micro messages of the face are instinctive. Reflect on a moment a child may have picked up on a nonverbal cue because he or she saw your true emotion or intention.

For instance, years ago, my then 5-year-old daughter said to me, "Mommy you look mad!" I replied, "I am not mad," to which she returned, "but your *face* looks mad." Listen with your eyes, as well as your ears (Young, 2007).

TIPS FOR NONVERBAL CUES AND COMMUNICATION

Recognize that people communicate on many levels, so you have to watch their body language: facial expressions, eye contact, and hand, foot, and body movements. Every gesture communicates something, and body expressions do not lie. If you study someone's movements, it only takes a few seconds to determine whether he or she is being truthful.

You can definitely improve your interpersonal communications and build more flourishing relationships by becoming more aware of other people's nonverbal cues and more cognizant of your own. This is especially important if the people you're trying to communicate with are very different from you. Most of us are open books when it comes to nonverbal cues. Multicultural differences in facial expressions, body placement, and—in particular—gestures are enormously open to misinterpretation. Let's examine a few more of these cues.

COMMUNICATION WITHOUT WORDS

- **Action language:** Movements that aren't used as signals but still send a message. These may include shaking someone's hand or giving the OK sign.
- **Chronemics:** Communication through the use of time. In some cultures, like in the United States for instance, promptness is highly valued. In others, time is not important.

- **Kinesics:** Communication through body language, such as a smile, eye contact, posture, or hand gesture.
- **Object language:** The intentional or unintentional display of material things, such as machines, implements, art, architectural structures, or clothing.
- **Proxemics:** Communication through the use of personal space. People in different cultures communicate more comfortably at various distances. In general, there are three ranges:
  - **Intimate:** The distance required for lovemaking or wrestling; a range of six to 18 inches.
  - **Personal:** Close: one-and-a-half to two-and-a-half feet; far: two-and-a-half to four feet.
  - **Social:** Close: four to seven feet; far: seven to 12 feet.
  - **Public:** 12 feet or more.
- **Haptics:** Communication through touch; can vary from person to person and culture to culture. In some cultures hugs are welcomed; in others, they are considered offensive. For business purposes, a nice firm handshake seems to be accepted worldwide.
- **Oculesics:** Communication through the eyes, which is typically involuntary. Research has shown that pupils enlarge when they see something pleasant and narrow when the viewer is offended.
- **Metacommunication:** Implied meaning that requires the listener to read between the lines. Metacommunication takes into account word choices and omissions or silence as tools for conveying messages.
- **Olfactics:** Communication through smell. An aroma, fragrance, or perfume may evoke emotions or spark a memory, so the smell of baked bread sends a different message than rotten eggs.
- **Paralanguage:** Considers voice volume, tempo, tone, and hesitations, such as "uhm" or "ah," as forms of communication. Silence is not necessarily golden.
- **Sign language:** A language system for the deaf in which numbers, words, and punctuation have been transformed into hand gestures.

LISTEN UP!

Listening skills are the foundation of how effectively we hear and understand what others think, feel, and have to say about themselves. Listening, just like nonverbal communication, requires us to hear more than just words; it requires us to interpret emotions and understand body language and the intention behind the words. Effective listening requires practice.

In the book *The 7 Habits of Highly Successful People*, author Stephen R. Covey (1989) shares that highly effective listening can transform our careers, lives, and relationships. Covey emphasizes the importance of not merely going through the mechanical responses that might be required for ordinary listening but to actually connect with the speaker's point of view so that you can empathize with how he or she is feeling. The only way to establish communication in professional and personal situations is by becoming, in small part, the person you are listening to—putting yourself in his or her shoes. Most of us are capable of listening at this level but rarely do it. Listening in order to become aware of the values and goals of others enables you to find common ground and maintain productive relationships (Covey, 1989).

Good listening skills are especially important when you're trying to make connections with people who are different. I'm not talking about letting the person speak so that you can then take your turn. Good listening skills require that you hear what the other person is saying and then take the time to probe further so you can give a meaningful response. Do this and the people you meet will be more likely to respond to you in a positive manner in the future.

BARRIERS TO LISTENING

There are times when we do our best to listen but some type of interference prevents us from focusing. If for some reason, you can't connect with someone, check your own listening skills and examine the environment for clues. Following are the top reasons you may not be listening effectively:
- You can't physically hear the speaker.
- The speaker's voice, rate of speech, accent, appearance, grammar usage, mannerisms, and pronunciation are distracting.
- You are preoccupied with your own thoughts.
- You and the speaker have a different understanding of certain words or phrases.
- The speaker is providing so many details that you're confused about the main point.
- You're turned off by the speaker's emotions.
- You think you know all there is to know about a certain subject.
- You don't believe the speaker knows what he or she is talking about.
- You consider the subject boring, complicated, or just plain uninteresting.
- You're sleepy, tired, hungry, or in a hurry and want to leave.
- You are preoccupied with another activity you need to tend.
- You're so focused on your response that you don't fully hear what the speaker is saying.
- Your attention is pulled to some other distraction in the room.

(Anastasia, 2015; Avery-Stoss, 2015)

So, what do you do if you find yourself in any of the above scenarios? Stop. Either ask the listener to repeat what he's said or ask to move to a setting more conducive to better communication. You might say, "Hey, it's a bit noisy (or hot) in here. Is it possible for us to talk outside?"

If you've had a hard day, let your speaker know and offer a better time to continue the conversation. Be honest. Also, get in the habit of repeating what the speaker has said to you during certain intervals in the conversation so he can confirm that he's been understood. What you don't want to do is pretend you've heard the speaker or pretend you've been listening if you haven't. That's no way to make a real connection.

PRESS THE RESET BUTTON: MAKING CONNECTIONS

Although you're bound to make some mistakes when attempting to develop relationships with people who are different from you, there are some things you can do to minimize misunderstandings and conflict, including:

- Avoid the use of idioms, slang expressions, and words that can have more than one meaning.
- Turn on your listening skills and don't be afraid to ask for clarification.
- Watch for nonverbal clues.
- Have an open mind and try not to judge.
- Give the other person the benefit of the doubt.

Developing new relationships can be stressful, but it can also be exciting and fun. You can become so adept at managing these relationships that you'll actually begin to enjoy meeting new people—whether they are Black, White, elderly, male, female, gay, or straight.

THE POWER OF WORDS

"People may hear your words, but they feel your attitude," so says author and leadership expert John C. Maxwell. Maxwell points out that it is not only important to recognize nonverbal cues and listening skills when communicating but also the words we use.

Word placement and sequence can make communication easier. These shortcuts, or prearranged "word packets," are often used in conversations in which we say what we think others want to hear rather than speaking the truth. People use word packets in developing relationships, especially with new acquaintances, because they are safe and comfortable. Word packets contain all the right words, so there is no conflict or challenge. For example: "It is so nice to meet you" or "Give me a call, and we will have lunch" (Young, 2007).

TAMING THE TONGUE

What's wrapped around the words you use? Our words are integrated with various thoughts, actions and experiences. Take a look at a few examples of the power of words as described by author Deborah Pegues in her 2005 book, *30 Days to Taming Your Tongue.*

- **Silent tongue:** Using silence as a means of expressing anger, retaliation, or displeasure, or not speaking up for fear of ridicule.
- **Know it all:** Tongue giving unsolicited input.
- **Hasty tongue:** Responding quickly with little consideration or thought.
- **Judgmental tongue:** Critical and faultfinding of another person's behavior.
- **Loquacious tongue:** Talking on and on and on.
- **Argumentative tongue:** Resisting anyone whose viewpoint is different from yours.

In addition to the words we use, how and where we talk to one another on a daily basis can also reveal a lot about who we really are (Pegues, 2005):
- **Hallway:** Surface talk; very little real conversation or listening; being polite.
- **Reporter:** Fact talk—what, where, who, how, why.
- **Intellectual:** Includes opinions, interpretations, or judgments.
- **Emotional:** How you feel about what you are saying.
- **Genuine:** Honest and open; not condemning, critical, or demanding.

ONCE UPON A TIME

While choosing words carefully is an important mechanism in developing and sustaining relationships, storytelling provides another bridge to make connections. The facts that we encounter have a tendency to be forgotten, but the stories we hear continue to make meaningful impressions. Stories offer a powerful vehicle to craft words, learn more about others, reveal information about ourselves, and help others understand our values and how we perceive life's experiences. (Wortmann, 2006).

What is more, well-told stories provide the opportunity to learn something we had not previously thought about or experienced, and teach us how we can move beyond the perceived barriers we encounter every day. (Wortmann, 2006).

STORYTELLER SOLEDAD O'BRIEN

In 2013 I had the opportunity to interview Soledad O'Brien, former anchor, special correspondent, and host of CNN's "Black in America" series during a visit to UNC-Charlotte. That same year, O'Brien released her critically acclaimed memoir *The Next Big Story: My Journey Through the Land of Possibilities*, which chronicles her biggest reporting moments and reveals how her upbringing and background influenced these experiences.

The daughter of a Black Cuban mother and a White Australian father, O'Brien grew up in the predominately white community of Long Island, New York. Even as a child O'Brien knew that she wanted to focus her career on telling the stories that may not otherwise be told.

As we spoke, O'Brien revealed her thoughts on the importance of storytelling as an educational tool. She says that storytelling gives voice to people who aren't often heard and tells tales that are sometimes overlooked. "I love telling people's stories and bringing their perspective and heart through storytelling," she said.

Storytelling can also put a "face" on an event, culture, or situation and make it clearer. For instance, in developing a story about women after the 9/11 crisis, O'Brien recalled how she initially encountered pushback from some producers who wanted to know why the story was important. She responded that the network had produced stories on the rescue attempts of men and dogs at the time, but none had been done on the women heroes of the tragic event. "We can put a face on their stories," O'Brien told the men.

"I learned that by putting a face on their stories we could all learn more from the experiences of 9/11—both triumph and tragedy." O'Brien also believes that sharing stories about diversity puts the United States in a unique position to demonstrate its multicultural population and viewpoints, especially since our country has a huge global impact. In addition to sharing experiences that expose our differences, however, stories offer a medium to expose that we are more alike than we often realize, despite gaps in lifestyles, education, and careers.

Stories come in all shapes, sizes, and colors, and provide multiple opportunities to learn about other human beings. Despite all of our idiosyncrasies, we're not as unique as we may believe. Stories can reveal this for us.

"Stories have to be told or they die, and when they die, we can't
remember who we are or why we're here."
—*SUE MONK KIDD, THE SECRET LIFE OF BEES*

MY THOUGHTS AND OBSERVATIONS

CHAPTER 8

ALWAYS CONNECTED; NEVER IN TOUCH

· ·

"It has become appallingly obvious that our technology has exceeded our humanity."

—ALBERT EINSTEIN

Flash back to the year 1997 and consider the digital world. There was no Google, much less Facebook, Instagram, YouTube, or Twitter. Smartphones, iPads, and tablets did not exist, and only a few adventurous people had found a date on match.com.

Today, there are more than 3.5 billion people online globally, with 83 percent being active users. Of these, 63 percent are between the ages of 18 and 54. This widespread usage has completely changed the way most of us access and share information. Just think how dramatically digital technology has evolved since the turn of the century:

- Facebook currently has more than 1.65 billion monthly users worldwide, while Twitter boasts 310 million monthly users.
- Sixty-eight percent of Americans own smartphones; 45 percent own tablets.
- Almost 5 billion people worldwide own cell phones.
- Anyone can become an instant news reporter via camcorder, cell phone, podcast, or YouTube.
- Print newspapers and magazines are dwindling, while their online counterparts are gaining momentum.
- E-books are giving conventional books the boot.
- There are 8 million blogs online, with 12,000 new blogs created each day.
- Grandparents connect with their grandchildren via e-mail and Skype.
- Teens use the Internet to challenge other Xbox players anywhere on the planet.
- One in four couples meets through online dating.
- Snapchat has more than 7 billion video views per day.
- There is no such thing as quitting time, since employees are accessible every minute of every day via the Internet or cell phone.
- Business cards include not only telephone numbers and addresses, but also Twitter and LinkedIn accounts, and e-mail and website addresses.

This chapter takes a look at how digital technology is used and how it should be used. It also addresses why digital communication can prove to be only an illusion when it comes to building relationships and facilitating friendships.

THE TECHNOLOGY ILLUSION

The evolution of digital technology has provided countless benefits, from connecting with others to accessing and publishing information, which allows us to contribute in ways never before possible. We can communicate with virtually anyone—anytime, anywhere. When the influence of online social media is added to the mix, the impact is far more reaching. In fact, these digital tools are so new, their influence won't be fully realized for years to come. One thing is certain: This new technology and the social media it supports make it virtually (no pun intended) impossible to avoid. You might as well be living on the moon if you're not connected to LinkedIn, Snapchat, Facebook, or Twitter.

These platforms allow us to gain inclusiveness and accessibility. They also remove barriers that can exist in face-to-face communication, such as voice volume and cadence, as well as body language (Tapscott, 2009). Since we can essentially be anyone we want behind our computer screens, we often present ourselves in ways that are most likable to the audience we're trying to impress. As humans, we have an innate desire to connect with others, and there's no substitute for that fundamental desire. Beyond this, we get real-time feedback, which can be powerful for making decisions and building relationships.

There are misuses as well. Digital technology can be addictive, taking precious time away from family, work, and social activities. Just as technology can give a false sense of security—or insecurity, as the case may be—it can also create an illusion of confidence, positive images, privacy, support, and resources. It is no wonder its utility has had an impact on all sorts of events, people, and places around the globe.

Take a look at the following examples:

- **The Arab Spring:** During the democratic uprisings that began in Tunisia in December 2010 and spread across the Arab world, social media was used to exchange information both domestically and globally. Social media did not, of course, cause the unrest nor instigate revolutions, but it did provide leaders and their followers a safe space to organize and gain support. It appears that Facebook played a role in mobilizing the younger, more urban, and digitally wired classes, giving them the comfort of an online community and making it feel safer to take collective action (Sourcewatch, 2015).

- **The Downfall of CIA Director David Petraeus:** Petraeus, a four-star army general, was forced to resign from the CIA after acknowledging he had revealed highly sensitive material to his biographer, Paula Broadwell. The two became involved in an affair that came to light after the

FBI investigated cyberstalking complaints issued by Tampa socialite Jill Kelley. The anonymous, harassing e-mails were eventually traced to Broadwell. There was no evidence of a security breach, but Broadwell had gained access to classified information as a result of what she routinely described as "unprecedented access to Petraeus." Although Petraeus used his personal e-mail account to communicate with Broadwell, not even the CIA director could hide his private electronic activities (Pearson, 2012).

- **Edward Snowden's National Security Agency Leaks.** Snowden, a former CIA employee, leaked classified information from the NSA in 2013 without prior authorization. The massive leak was the worst security breach in American history. Snowden's disclosures and the ensuing media coverage revealed the blueprints for numerous government surveillance programs, including those of U.S. allies (Braun, 2014).

- **Target Corporation's Data Breach:** Cyberthieves stole credentials from one of the retailer's vendors in order to access its system—according to forensic investigations into a data breach that may have exposed information from as many as 110 million customers. The breach included security codes and payment, debit card numbers, and personal information, such as names and home and e-mail addresses. The Target breach, which affected shoppers from November 27, 2013, to December 15, 2013, was the single largest retail data breach in history (Hamilton & Lopez, 2014; Hsu, 2014).

THE DARK SIDE OF TECHNOLOGY: TRUTH OR EXAGGERATION?

Despite the information readily available concerning the repercussions of the digital world, some people are still unclear about how technology can and should be used. The lines of personal and business conduct are blurred more and more frequently, especially considering that more than two-thirds of American adults use social media. Even former Secretary of State Hillary Clinton has used her personal e-mail account for government communication.

Digital communication poses additional problem for businesses. On June 2, 2016, Bank of America issued a public statement after one of its employees posted racist comments on Facebook. This was two weeks after the Wells Fargo Championship's Twitter account deleted tournament attendees sporting fake mustaches and sombreros on Cinco de Mayo.

"People seem to behave differently on social media than in their interpersonal relationships," stated employment law attorney Jonathan Crotty about the Bank of America incident. "And when it comes to your career ... it really isn't any different." (Charlotte Observer, p. 1 , 2016).

THE DARK SIDE

According to Don Tapscott, an expert on the economic and social impact of the digital revolution, especially for the Millennials and the Net generation, there are many concerns with the digital and technology explosion:

- **Dumbing down:** People aren't reading books because they can readily go to a search engine like Google and get information. They also have a hard time focusing and are easily distracted.
- **Loss of social skills:** Called "screenagers," net-addicted individuals spend hours and hours online. The idea of having face-to-face conversations is foreign to them.
- **No filters; no shame:** Digital displays of affection or provocative pictures are put out there for the world to see. There is a lack of understanding privacy online.
- **Lack of independence:** People have been coddled and are afraid to make decisions and cope by themselves.
- **Cheating and stealing information:** Intellectual property rights are easily violated. People share anything, with no respect for the creators or original owners. Plagiarism is rampant.
- **Bullying and violence:** Living in a virtual reality has created a culture of violence and humiliation, sometimes for fame.
- **Self-gratification:** People often have a sense of entitlement and exhibit attention-seeking behavior through digital communication.
- **Valueless individuals:** Individuals do not have sustained beliefs.

THE TRUTH

- **Dumbing down:** Individuals are not being dumbed down in terms of how they learn. Emerging evidence reveals that members of the Net generation are adapting to their wired world. New literacy models are being developed in which people have to be able to critique the information they are reading as valid or not. Technology is actually helping create other forms of education.
- **No filters; no shame:** Although research data suggests that social skills may suffer, technology and social media networks offer a different platform to create communities with friends, classmates, and relatives. Instant messaging allows you to think about what you are saying before you say it, and the platform has allowed individuals to do more things together. People are more socially connected day and night.
- **Lack of independence:** Many individuals give up their privacy when using online communication and do not really understand the consequences. Sharing everything—pictures, stories, comments,

thoughts, ideas, and fears—creates a heightened level of openness that can impact future jobs, promotions, and public service opportunities. It is a huge and unresolved issue.

- **Cheating and stealing information:** Not only is it easier for students to cheat or steal online, but many do not view their actions as inappropriate behavior. The historical model of owning and selling music or movies, for example, may be outdated and require the need for new distribution methods. In the future, explicit rules and regulations for social media, intellectual property rights, confidentiality clauses, and security protocols will affect the integrity of decisions on digital materials and information.

- **Bullying and violence:** There are terrible examples of bullying and violence online, and compelling evidence and data that suggest there is a direct link between online activities and these instances. Exposing violent acts can assist in identifying perpetrators and be used to educate the public, but such exposure can backfire when copycats get in on the act. Bullies need an audience, and the Internet provides just what they need. Cyberbullies can target individuals anywhere, anytime, with no time constraints. That is why the Internet is so attractive. Understanding the human behavior underlying this problem will help develop effective strategies to combat it.

- **Self-gratification:** Has digital communication created a space for individuals to believe "it is all about me?" For example, Instagram is a free online photo-sharing social network platform used to "capture and share the world's moments." You can post photos of yourself with family, friends, and those who follow you, who also get the opportunity to "like" your pictures. What you say and do is also the center of attention on Twitter, although using 140 characters does not leave much room for specific details.

- **Valueless individuals:** Have values changed because of technology? It is easy to see from the preceding examples that many have, but there have been positive influences as well. The Net generation values family and friends, and participation in community service and volunteerism is at an all-time high.

VIRTUAL COMMUNICATION

Digital technology is so prevalent that many people believe the connections made through devices are on par with those made through physical contact. However, seeing another person on a computer screen or reading updates posted on a blog will never be as fulfilling as seeing someone in person.

Philanthropist Melinda Gates addressed this subject during a May 2013 graduation address she presented to students at Duke University. "Technology is just a tool. It's a powerful tool, but it's just a tool," she said. "Deep human connection is different. It's not a tool. It's not a means to an end. It is the end—the purpose and the result of a meaningful life—and it will inspire the most amazing acts of love, generosity and humanity."

Blogger Tom Schramski agrees. "Everyone is using technology, but it can be a barrier because it is a different type of communication process," he explains. "Face-to-face communication provides an opportunity for a higher level of interaction. When you are actually talking on the phone, which is becoming more obsolete, it is easier to make connections that will lead to a foundation for relationships to develop." Communication-related technology can be invaluable, but face-to-face communication is the foundation for most long-term relationships (Schramski, 2013).

Online communication also acts as a shield from which you can make anonymous posts on a variety of topics and issues without suffering consequences. People share memories and experiences with ease in the digital community, but it cannot replace talking and person-to-person interaction (White, 2013).

Some of the things that make people special can't be translated in a technological space. Knowing someone is not the same as reading the contents of his online profile. Seeing someone on Skype is not the same as seeing someone in person. For me, Skype is a different version of talking on the telephone. Sure, it allows an exchange of information, but you miss a lot of communication that occurs through body language, facial expressions, voice inflections, or the impact of a shared environment.

Another thing you may not realize is that the digital messages you receive are not as personal as you may believe. Websites like Facebook and Twitter, for example, utilize applications that send automated postings. So, if you're a recipient of these messages, the person you've befriended or the one you've chosen to follow is not necessarily behind the posting. Some people also subcontract their social media activities to either a virtual assistant or a social media management company.

ARE YOU FOR REAL?

Let's look at the technological friendship model. Can you really have a best friend that you've never met in person? Absolutely not. According to *Merriam-Webster*, a *friend* is "a person attached to another by feelings of affection or personal regard" (n.d.). A friend is a confidant. There is nothing confidential about technological friendship. Some people argue that they have deep personal technology-based friendships because they share intimate details of their lives and oftentimes receive instant feedback.

The word *friend*, however, is overused. People buy into the notion that those they connect with on Facebook or follow on Twitter are friends. We've oversimplified the definition of what a true friend is in order to keep people in our lives, even if it's on artificial terms. Though technology can be a starting point, it can't replace the work that needs to be done to fully cultivate long-lasting relationships.

Twitter provides a totally new perspective because you "follow" people to see what they are doing every second. As a receiver, you may feel the person sending tweets is speaking directly to you, maintaining an intimate relationship; however, the tweeter may have goals that don't concern you, disseminating details for his or her own purposes. When a celebrity like Kim Kardashian or Beyoncé tweets personal information about what they are doing—dining at a restaurant, shopping, or attending a meeting—the recipients feel special. The truth is they may be tweeting simply to get followers excited enough about their activities to buy their brands or watch their television programs.

Social media can become a crutch that allows individuals to peek into each other lives without having them directly in your personal space. It is easy to craft an image with tweets, updates, and pictures to cultivate an online persona (Jue, Marr, & Kassotakis, 2010).

FACE OFF

Let's examine Facebook. Nearly half a billion people use Facebook every day, so it's vital that we understand the consequences of that usage on our well-being. "Giving people the power to share and make the world more open and connected" (n.d.) is Facebook's mission, but a recent study indicates the social network site may leave users feeling powerless and disconnected instead.

A study published August 14, 2013, on the website PLOS ONE revealed that researchers text messaged college-aged participants five times per day for two weeks, asking questions about loneliness, anxiety, and emotional well-being. They discovered that the more people used Facebook, the worse they felt the next time they received a text message, and the more they used Facebook over a two-week period, the more their life satisfaction levels declined over time.

The reason for their unhappiness? Social comparison. Since people generally post about what they're doing, especially when they're having fun, those observing on Facebook may feel their lives are lacking in some way, leading to sadness and dissatisfaction with life. Furthermore, "constant texting allows a false sense of validation and feeds a feeling that we can't be alone. I share therefore I am" (Turkle, 2011, p. 180-181).

And there's another side to Facebook: It can spell disaster if participants are irresponsible. A 2009 UCLA study found that the switching of focus back and forth from work to communicating leads to both an inability to absorb information and a decline in critical thinking and decision-making skills (Town & Country Living Social Graces, 2011).

An article published in the *Tech Journal* cited Facebook as the new cause of divorce. According to the author, 20 percent of divorce petitions reference Facebook as the root cause of marital mayhem and/or as evidence to incriminate the cheating spouse. Inappropriate sexual chats appear to be the most common Facebook misuse by unscrupulous husbands and wives (Das, 2009).

A June 6, 2013, article on the *Huffington Post* further documented this research. Russell Clayton cited that those who checked Facebook more than hourly are "more likely to experience Facebook-related conflict with their romantic partners and cause negative relationship outcomes, including physical and emotional cheating." This is the most pronounced in newer relationships.

Some take their virtual flirtations further, making them quite costly in the long run. These cheaters don't realize that their racy photos, steamy chats, personal online postings, Facebook and MySpace pages (one of the earliest social media platforms), and intimate confessions can be used against them in divorce proceedings.

Just ask Congressman Chris Lee. The married senator responded to a Craigslist ad posted by a 34-year-old woman who was looking for a man. Lee responded with a series of e-mails through which he provided a shirtless picture of himself, lied about his age and marital status (he claimed he was divorced), and said he was a lobbyist rather than revealing his true position in Congress. Lee was busted by the media when the e-mails were traced to his Facebook account. As a result, he resigned from Congress.

Congressman Anthony Weiner was forced to resign a short time later after he posted lewd photographs of himself to the Twitter account he used to communicate with his constituents. Nothing is private—or sacred when it comes to digital technology. There is also an illusion that what gets posted remains in the confines of the Facebook space. However, if you were to read the terms of service, you'd see that whatever you post becomes the property of Facebook and can be used for its purposes. Terms of service can be changed at any time without user permission. Other sites, such as spokeo.com, use Facebook data to compile personal details about users. In addition to contact information, this profile may include relatives, credit scores, and home values.

A FALSE REALITY

We live in a culture in which digital devices are the core of how millions of people daily communicate. Market researcher and author Martin Lindstrom discovered how deeply affected individuals can become while interacting with technology. His research showed that many people feel the same way about their cell phones as they do their best friends. When subjects saw or heard their phones ringing, the neurons in their brains associated those feelings with love and compassion. This means these neurons crossed the distinctions between seeing and doing. Technology has capitalized on this process to create a reality in which objects, such as cellphones or digital communication such as tweets or Facebook likes, feel like real relationships and interactions.

The 2014 PBS Frontline documentary *Generation Like* explores how younger populations are selling, showing, and marketing themselves online. Author and media, technology, and culture researcher

Douglas Rushoff reveals in this documentary how the economy uses the currency of "likes." It is good to be liked. It is good to like things and associate those likes with being more liked.

In *Generation X to Z: Teens and the New Cool*, Alissa Quart questions how these generations are making authentic connections. In an effort to increase their Facebook numbers, they like everything and friend everyone. "If everyone is a Facebook friend, what is an actual friend?" she asks. Futhermore, do they really know or understand what a friend is? This is a result of both a data-rich and socially networked world (Quart, 2013; Ruskoff, 2014).

In Dale Carnegie's *New York Times* bestseller *How to Win Friends and Influence People*, Carnegie states that people are "always connected but never in touch," and that's the illusion technology promotes. Originally published in 1936, with more than 15 million copies sold worldwide, the book offers six ways to get people to like you, which include: becoming genuinely interested in others; smiling; remembering other people's names; being a good listener; encouraging others to talk about themselves; and making other people feel important. These tenets cannot effectively and efficiently be accomplished through technology. If you look at platforms such as Facebook, LinkedIn, and Twitter, you will notice that the posts are designed for self-promotion, which is quite contrary to the points made in Carnegie's book.

"Parasocial interactions" mean we have to switch on the Instagram, television, computer, iPad, smartphone, or Internet to feel connected, despite knowing logically this is not real human contact (Greenwood, p. 57). Even the popular dating site match.com knows the difference. In addition to initial online meetings, the company has created Match Events, in which individuals can meet face-to-face in secure locations, truly providing another level of interaction for developing relationships.

REBOOT YOUR THINKING

If you truly want to cultivate relationships with people who are different from yourself, you need to understand that technology is just one aspect of the friendship. It's OK to send an e-mail, tweet, or post, but you can't fully rely on these for a textured relationship. Old-fashioned networking and relationship-building exercises are relevant, even in this technological age. Additionally, your use of technology needs to be authentic. The information you share on every platform should be consistent with the image you want to portray. Technology can hide your character flaws, lies, morality issues, or poor core values only for so long.

Since everything is connected, at some point you should expect your true self to be revealed. You need to ensure that the "technological you" is the same as the one your friends and family know. If that's not the case, then you need to make a change. How does your technology use relate to nurturing extraordinary, diverse relationships? First, you need to understand that participating in digital communication is risky, but if done effectively and responsibly, can be the basis for amazing connections you can further facilitate offline.

Next, you need to realize that when people view your smart use of technology, they'll have a clearer picture of who you are, and that will enable you to foster richer and more honest communications in the real world. According to Sherry Turkle, author of *Alone Together: Why We Expect More From Technology and Less From Each Other*, we need to be aware of the impact of technology. It has "created this constant pressure to respond. This anxiety is part of the new community of connectivity. It telegraphs an expectation that we are efficient; we are available 24/7" (2011, p. 95). Higher levels of diverse relationships can be developed if you disconnect from technology long enough to indulge in a higher level of diverse relationships. Start by reviewing the information below:

- Examine your Facebook connections. Do most of them look like you? If the site remained true to its original intent, which was to give Ivy League students a platform to connect, then most members would probably look similar to its founder, Mark Zuckerberg. Since membership has expanded to include almost everyone over age 13 on the planet, the social networking site provides access to people of every nationality, culture, and race. To date, Facebook has more than 1.65 billion monthly users worldwide, with around 75 percent of the U.S. population participating in a Facebook account. Conceivably, your Facebook connections could and should represent the great American melting pot.

- If you're networking in online communities like LinkedIn effectively, your list should include a diverse group of professionals. For example, personal development groups, such as bowling leagues, garden clubs, or self-defense classes, allow you to have fun. Expand your links. All of these encounters have value, according to Donald Trump. This wildly successful entrepreneur says that you should "spend a portion of every day working on personal development. It's just as important as the time you spend building your business" (Turkle, 2011, p. 180–181).

THE OBAMA EFFECT

According to Don Tapscott, a leading authority on innovation, media and the economic and social impact of technology, "The Obama Effect" was the first transmedia political campaign of the 21st century in which engaging two-way technologies, including mobile devices, laptops, iPads and tablets, smartphones, and social networking sites became as important as traditional media. The campaign's social networking site gave proponents the opportunity to build support, hold rallies, raise money, and develop a sense of community. The donor experience involved confirmations and thank-you notes, connecting ordinary citizens to the success of the campaign. This people-power in action was different from the traditional top-down political campaign system.

E-mails served as a primary platform for sending relevant information and campaign updates. The former senator had followers and followed others on Facebook and Twitter. His digital campaign recognized the need for entertainment and speed, making supporters feel they had an immediate connection with the future president. This connection opened the door for supporters to see President Obama as transparent and, ultimately, someone they felt they could trust (Tapscott, 2009).

"If you want to understand the new connected world and how we choose to live in it—look no further than our Internet behavior; after all, we are what we Click!"
—*BILL TANCER*

MY THOUGHTS AND OBSERVATIONS

_____

_____

_____

_____

_____

_____

_____

_____

_____

_____

_____

_____

CHAPTER 9

WHEN YOU KNOW BETTER, YOU DO BETTER

"Now That I Know Better, I Do Better,"

—*MAYA ANGELOU*

During the writing of this manuscript Dr. Maya Angelou passed away, but she left us with countless pieces of wisdom. In one of her many interviews, Angelou discussed how we perceive differences. She said that our thoughts do not begin in a vacuum; they are all around us. Feelings such as racism are in the grass and trees, in our homes, furniture, and clothes, and they finally move into our very beings.

Thoughts and assumptions develop as a fabric of who we are, infiltrating us, often as a result of our family history. But we do not have to retain those beliefs. We can be intentional about making changes in our story, and when you know better, you do better! *What Color Are Your Jellybeans?* has suggested various activities you can participate in to begin the process of improving your relationships. Remember, it is OK to acknowledge that you do not know everything about developing diverse relationships.

During the recent PBS documentary *African American Lives*, the narrator poignantly shared his personal experience of watching the program. He was not taught much of the material in school; neither was it discussed in his home. "There are lots of things about history I was not taught, but that does not mean I cannot still learn about these areas of history in my 60s" (Gates, 2014), he said.

We are not born with feelings of indifference, hatred, or racism. Those are learned behaviors. In the same manner we learned those feelings, we must educate ourselves to do the right thing in regard to humanity. But there are no easy steps. Education is a process. One workshop, training session, lunch-and-learn, or conference can jump-start the process, but these alone are not enough to provide a foundation for intentional changes.

LESSONS FROM SHANGHAI

Cultural blind spots often keep us from seeing the true nature of those from other countries, but what if you could immerse yourself in another culture firsthand? Would you be able to adapt and excel in unfamiliar surroundings? Andrew Ballen may not be a familiar name, but he serves as the perfect example of an expatriate successfully living and learning another culture. A Black man of Jamaican and American descent, Ballen has become one of the most recognized faces in Shanghai, China, due to his popular internationally aired travel show *Getaway*. The founder and CEO of Shanghai-based AVD Digital Media, as well as a Millennial marketing expert, Ballen is known in China as "Da Long" (大龙), or "Big Dragon."

After leaving prestigious Duke University Law School, Ballen became an accidental entrepreneur, when, after his arrival in Shanghai, he developed several highly successful businesses. They ranged from hip-hop parties and elaborate events to radio and television shows, as well as China's first interactive video shopping experience for Nike. Although Ballen's initial motivation was to show his family that he could be a success no matter where he was in the world, he exceeded that goal many times.

When he reached China, Ballen was forced to learn the language, and he became fluent in Mandarin. While traveling the country, Ballen saw parts of China that many Chinese had not visited; and he learned details about the Chinese culture—such as the importance of family and music—beyond what he could find on the Internet or read about in books. This cultural immersion proved to be at the core of his future business success. Although you may not be able to uproot your life to have an experience like Andrew Ballen, his example reveals the power of moving beyond one's self to open the door for others to be a part of your life. But even you're an armchair traveler, there's plenty to learn.
(Smiley, 2011; Zachery, 2005).

EDUCATION IS THE KEY

Dr. Beverly Daniel-Tatum (1997) wrote one my favorite books, *Why Are All the Black Kids Sitting Together in the Cafeteria?* In the book, she discusses that when teachers, administrators, and staff walk into racially mixed high schools, they instantly notice identifiable groups of ethnic students—Black, Latino, or Asian students—sitting together in the cafeteria. The irony is they rarely mention or ask, "Why are all the White kids sitting together?"

Knowing better begins with self-education. According to Daniel-Tatum (1997), it is important to understand how you are educated about individuals who are different from you. You learn the assumptions you make about others at an early age. Even in our preschool years, we are exposed to misinformation—or no information at all. Many people grow up in neighborhoods in which there is limited exposure or opportunity to interact with people who are different from their own families. Although they may not personally engage in inequality or bigotry firsthand, these differences are woven into the fabric of society.

According to education, multiculturalism, and diversity expert Dr. Roslyn Mickelson (2014), diversity impacts academic achievement. Students benefit from diversity because it promotes higher graduation rates, allays the fears of interacting with people who are different, promotes friendship across cultural divides, deters involvement in the criminal justice system and, most importantly, better prepares young people to work in a diverse work environment.

All students learn more in diverse settings with peers from other racial, ethnic, and socioeconomic backgrounds. Diversity in the classroom provides the foundation for unity and strength within our communities. Adults who are educated in diverse settings are more likely to:

- live in integrated neighborhoods
- have friends from many races and ethnic groups
- be employed in diverse workplaces (Mickelson, 2014; R. A. Mickelson, interview, April 14, 2012).

IT'S NEVER TOO LATE

In a tribute to Martin Luther King during the last year of the *Oprah Winfrey Show*, Oprah revisited a guest from 1989. James Rainey was a vocal racist who did not like Black people—or other people of color. He felt that Blacks and people of color should stay in their place; and if they failed to do so, he would use violent measures to keep them in check.

Without warning, though, the unthinkable happened to a member of his family. Rainey's daughter got pregnant by a young African American man. Rainey was so enraged he had to restrain himself from committing a crime. However, once his grandchild was born, he had an epiphany. He realized that the baby didn't care about White or Black; all his grandson saw was the grandpa he loved.

The birth of Rainey's grandson transformed Rainey from a bigoted man once filled with hate, prejudice, and bias into a man of love and compassion. Rainey later adopted two African American boys and is raising them with his wife. According to Rainey, the secret to changing how you relate to people is to "get beyond what you *see* so you can embrace the humanity in all of us. … I once could not do that but now, more than 30 years later, I chose to change."

The multiracial population around the world is increasing. It is projected that by 2050, one in five Americans will be mixed race. Educating yourself about people who are different benefits everyone. It's never too late to change.

WHAT IS CULTURE?

The term *culture* still abounds with confusion. Sometimes the term is used to denote a group of people in regard to race or ethnicity with a shared history; other times it has been exclusively linked to ethnicity or race. However, most people belong to more than one culture. People with white skin do not belong to one culture, just as people with black or yellow skin do not all belong to one culture. They all have differences that make each unique.

Culture has also been used to explain the connections between groups of people—like a glue that holds them together. The term is often used as if groups are homogeneous, not taking into account the diversity among the individuals in that group. Have you ever tried sorting someone's race or culture by looking at them? Visit https://www.pbs.org/race/002_SortingPeople/002_00-home.htm and test your knowledge.

REFERENCE

Tong, R. (2011). Multicultural and global feminisms. In B. J. Bank (Ed.), Gender and higher education (pp. 71–77). Baltimore: Johns Hopkins University Press.

"Preservation of one's own culture does not require contempt or disrespect
for other cultures."
—*CESAR CHAVEZ*

MY THOUGHTS AND OBSERVATIONS

CHAPTER 10

JUST DO IT!

• •

"You and I are virtually identical to one another at the level of our genes. "

—JILL BOLTE TAYLOR, PH.D.

If you still believe that developing relationships with people who are different from you is just a nice thing to do, then you have missed the point of this book. The face of America is changing. The face of our world is changing. If you're unable to facilitate connections with people who are different, you will be left behind. You could be excluded from opportunities that you won't even know exist.

At this point, the jellybeans in your cup should include all the colors of the rainbow, or you should at least have a plan to start the transformation. I provided the tools. First, you discovered how to identify differences among people and how to handle them. You received tips on how to move past your fears when it comes to relationships. You learned when you should and should not use technology in connecting with people who are different, released any ideas you had about weirdness and normality, and were provided with evidence that the differences among humans are minute and that observation alone should make relationship building easier.

I believe there is no more noble a calling than helping people of the world live together in peace and understanding. This is not an easy task, and it requires each of us to become fully aware of our own culture. It also demands that we build skills in developing and maintaining relationships with people from various cultures, which are often dramatically different from our own. The material in this book was designed to assist you and your organization in accomplishing this feat.

What Color Are Your Jellybeans? offers the opportunity to explore a simple question- and-answer process to help you determine how to interact on a daily basis with those different from you. Regardless of where you fall on the scale of diverse relationships, there is always room for improvement. As long as you commit to change and take action, you're on your way to designing extraordinary relationships. Just continue forging ahead—and remember there's no time like the present.

NOW WHAT?

Fulfilling relationships fuel your personal and professional efforts. The insight in this guide can be integrated in your everyday life. Hopefully, your life and the lives of others will be enriched by these concepts. You know it's possible to master the art of diverse relationship building. Prepare a power-packed action plan and forge ahead.

DEDICATION

This book is dedicated to my 90-year-old grandmother, who demonstrated that you can develop extraordinary relationships with those different from you at any age. My African American grandmother cultivated a friendship with another octogenarian—a White woman, Miss Louise, who lived directly across the street. Miss Louise passed away last year but their friendship was something I thought I would never witness. Her daughter now comes to see my grandmother. During her lifetime, my grandmother encountered on a daily basis some of the harshest prejudice you could imagine. She lived in the very racially divided town of Danville, Virginia, where, for the most part, Black people and White people lived in completely separate neighborhoods.

For many decades, my grandmother was the first and only African American seamstress for the Belk store in town. As such, she endured the racial slurs of coworkers and customers alike. While colleagues ignored her for the most part, they enjoyed taking credit for her accomplished work. They also required my grandmother to redo her coworkers' mistakes—without recognition. You would think she would be bitter; instead she saw past their insults and opened her eyes to their humanity. I don't know that I could have been that open-minded or forgiving, but it does help prove to me that anything is possible. I hope my granny's tale motivates you, as well, to shoot for the stars as you strive for extraordinary relationships.

"What a wonderful kind of day. If we could learn to work and play
and get along with each other."
—*MARC BROWN, FROM THE THEME SONG OF ARTHUR*

"Seeking and learning are in fact nothing but recollection."
—*PLATO*

MY THOUGHTS AND OBSERVATIONS

_____

_____

_____

_____

_____

_____

_____

_____

_____

_____

_____

CHAPTER 11

COMMIT TO LONG-TERM CHANGE!

• •

"The real voyage of discovery is not seeking new landscapes, but in having a new eye."

—MARCEL PROUST

Are you ready to commit to embracing differences? If you know you're committed to long-term change, the following activities will aid you on beginning or enhancing your journey on developing extraordinary relationships. Have fun!

50 POWER-PACKED ACTIONS TO HELP YOU JUMP-START AND DEVELOP EXTRAORDINARY RELATIONSHIPS

1. Host an international Thanksgiving holiday with the folks at your office or in your neighborhood, depending on which group is more diverse.
2. Get together with your international friends for a round-robin dinner party. One person in the group hosts the appetizers, another hosts the main course, and another, desserts. The group moves from house to house (usually close in proximity), indulging in a variety of ethnic foods. Of course, the host plays her country's traditional music and may even wear relevant attire to set the mood.
3. Volunteer with the Special Olympics: http://www.specialolympics.org/volunteers.aspx.
4. Visit the U.S. Memorial Holocaust Museum. The museum in Washington, D.C., features exhibits that pay tribute to Holocaust victims. Visit http://www.ushmm.org or call (202) 488-0400.
5. Check out the Diversity Pride website. Though the site focuses on events for the gay, lesbian, bisexual, transgender, and intersex communities, all activities are open to straight parents, friends, family, and allies of gays as well. Visit https://www.genderspectrum.com
6. Take an ethnic cooking class. Many restaurants, community colleges, cookware shops, and even fitness centers offer a variety of cooking classes. If you're feeling really ambitious, take an

authentic Thai cooking class at the Royal Thai Cuisine in Bangkok. Visit https://www.viator.com/Bangkok/d343-ttd

7. Attend an international music festival. These feature a variety of musical genres and are held in locations throughout the world. Check out http://www.musicfestivalwizard.com.

8. Subscribe to *DiversityInc*, a bold magazine that offers thought-provoking commentary on diversity issues, as well as the popular column *Ask the White Guy*. Visit http://www.DiversityInc.com.

9. Host an international game night. Invite people from various cultures to your home or community center, and ask them to bring a popular game from their native country. After the games are explained, the group chooses which ones they want to play. Enjoy hors d'oeuvres from around the world as you interact.

10. Volunteer abroad. International Volunteer HQ and International Volunteer Programs Abroad are two organizations that offer opportunities to volunteer in developing nations, where you can get firsthand exposure to different cultures while helping others. Visit http://www.volunteerhq.org or http://www.volunteerinternational.org.

11. Work in a soup kitchen. These organizations are often in need of help, particularly during the holidays.

12. Take or teach a course at your local library. The library is a great place to meet a variety of people—and if you have a particular skill, share your expertise.

13. Be a pen pal. PenPal World has more than 870,000 global members. The site offers a free limited account that allows visitors to contact and reply to up to three members within 24 hours. Visit www.penpalworld.com.

14. Encourage diversity with your children through reading. Two books to add to your list are *It's Okay to Be Different* by Todd Parr and *Whoever You Are* by Mem Fox.

15. Ring in the Chinese New Year by hosting a celebration or attending one. Visit https://www.viator.com/Bangkok/d343-ttd.

16. Host a movie viewing at your home, followed by a discussion. Invite a variety of people and start with Chris Rock's documentary, *Good Hair*.

17. Learn a new language. Take a course at a local college or international house.

18. Visit your city's international house and learn about ways you can get involved. It's the perfect place to experience a new culture with no travel involved.

19. Go Irish. Attend some of the nation's largest St. Patrick's Day parades, such as the one in New York City, Chicago, or Savannah, Georgia.

20. Visit the United Nations. Experience international diplomacy firsthand. Headquartered in New York City on First Avenue between 42nd and 48th Streets, the U.N. is open daily with a

few exceptions in and around the holidays. English-speaking tours are offered every 30 minutes. Call (212) 963-8687.

21. Visit. Visit Bertha's Kitchen's in North Charleston, SC; Gullah Grub in St. Helena Islands and Jestine's Kitchen to experience the different cuisine of Soul Food; Gullah Cooking; Low Country and Southern Cooking. Visit http://discoversouthcarolina.com/articles/southern-lowcountry-gullah-or-soul-whats-the-difference-between-these-sc-cooking-styles.

22. Google "global and international" with your hobbies and find interesting groups to join. Essence.com August 2016

23. Keep a diversity journal. Write about the diverse activities you have been participating in and how they have impacted your impressions of the people you've met, as well as your worldview.

24. Organize a caroling event. Be sure to feature holiday songs that represent the different nationalities in your neighborhood.

25. Teach in Thailand: The Teach and Travel Project through the American TESOL Institute has an amazing teaching opportunity. Candidates accepted into the program are guaranteed a short-term ESL job in Thailand paying approximately $1,000 USD per month, plus housing and medical insurance. Visit http://www.gviusa.com.

26. Visit the King Center in Atlanta. Established in 1968 by Dr. Martin Luther King, Jr.'s wife, Coretta Scott King, the King Center is the official, living memorial to the man who led the Civil Rights Movement in America. The center features exhibits and artifacts in tribute to his legacy. Call (404) 526-8900 or visit http://www.thekingcenter.org.

27. Soothe your baby with music from around the globe. *Dreamland: World Lullabies & Soothing Songs* features relaxing tunes from Africa, Scotland, Argentina, Japan, and a host of other countries. Available on Amazon.

28. Learn about your own ancestry. Learning your ancestral history will help you develop an understanding and appreciation of your own cultural background. Check out http://www.ancestry.com to begin.

29. Do a self-directed study on a global diversity issue, such as women and work, or the economies of third-world countries. This type of study allows you to see beyond typical information sources to discover how issues affect people around the world. Some ideas for the study include researching through the international section of a library or interviewing members of a special-interest chamber of commerce, such as one for Latinos or Asians. Share your knowledge with friends and colleagues through a newsletter, blog, or e-mail.

30. Host a virtual coffee with someone around the world. As long as you and your international coffee friend have Skype, you can enjoy your virtual cup of joe free.

31. Participate in a mission trip. There are numerous opportunities through houses of worship or organizations such as the American Red Cross to help those in need.

32. Learn sign language. You can teach yourself with a book or contact the American Sign Language resource site for teacher referrals. Visit http://www.lifeprint.com.

33. Run with the bulls—or just watch the action. The *encierro* is a practice in which people run through the streets in front of a small group of bulls that have been let loose. Though the most famous running of the bulls happens annually from July 6 to July 14 in Pamplona, Spain, during the seven-day festival of Sanfermines in honor of San Fermin, this activity is also held in other villages and towns throughout Spain, Mexico, and Portugal. Be aware there are between 200 and 300 people injured each year—and several deaths—so run at your own risk.

34. Visit Puebla, Mexico, during Cinco de Mayo. You'll see firsthand how the country commemorates the Mexican army's unlikely victory over France in 1862. Celebrated on May 5, Cinco de Mayo is a time during which Mexican culture and history are widely showcased and appreciated. http://www.mexonline.com/cinco-de-mayo.htm

35. Jump up during the Trinidad and Tobago Carnival. Known for its music, dancing, and fanfare, this official Caribbean festival is the inspiration for similar celebrations worldwide. Visit http://www.gotrinidadandtobago.com/trinidad/carnival.

36. Take a Gullah tour. Gullah is the language spoken by the original Black inhabitants of the Charleston/Beaufort, South Carolina, region. The tour showcases the culture, places, history, stories, and contributions that are meaningful to Black Charlestonians.

37. Discover how other cultures celebrate or bury their dead. You can start by reading *Death and Bereavement Across Cultures*, edited by Colin Murray Parkes, Pittu Laungani, and Bill Young; *Death, Mourning, and Burial: A Cross-Cultural Reader*, edited by Antonius C.G.M. Robben (part of *The Human Lifecycle: Cross-Cultural Readings*); *Chinese American Death Rituals: Respecting the Ancestors*, edited by Sue Fawn Chung and Priscilla Wegars; and *Remembering Well: Rituals for Celebrating Life and Mourning Death*, by Sarah York.

38. Volunteer with Habitat for Humanity. There are various programs that you can support, but the two that appear to provide the most comprehensive worldwide perspective include: 1) Habitat for Humanity Global Village, which enables you to travel to places like Zambia, Macedonia, Mongolia, and Alaska for two-week stints, and 2) the International Volunteer Program, which allows you to serve with one of their overseas offices for several months. Visit http://www.habitat.org/ivp.

39. Host a birthday party for homeless children. Since 2005, Bright Blessings in Charlotte, North Carolina, has been hosting birthday parties for homeless children and their families. The effort

has grown into a full-blown organization that hosts numerous programs for homeless families. Your area may have such an organization as well. Visit http://www.brightblessingsusa.org.

40. Take your spouse to a Weekend to Remember getaway. Though this retreat is unlikely to come to a locale near you sometime soon, consider a place that's not exactly in your backyard. That way you'll have a chance to connect with your spouse in a new environment, scratch a desired destination off your bucket list, and connect with people you wouldn't ordinarily meet. Visit http://www.familylife.com.

41. Dance away your diversity hang-ups. Take salsa, swing, or ballroom dancing lessons. Your moves aren't the focus; you just want to choose a dance that you're willing to learn and commit to having fun. Don't forget to invite your friends.

42. Expose your youngsters to literature that features children with disabilities. Two works include *Catherine's Story* by Genevieve Moore, a book about a young girl's experiences with epilepsy; and *A Screaming Kind of Day* by Rachna Gilmore, which features a hearing-impaired girl's challenges.

43. Host an international student. Give students an opportunity to learn about your culture while you learn about theirs. Check for opportunities with your house of worship, local international house, or English-language school, or visit (http://www.academicyear.org/landing/bing.asp?utm_source=bing&utm_medium=cpc&utm_campaign=SIG)

44. Volunteer to serve on a multicultural committee in your community. Be on the lookout for Greek festivals, Cinco de Mayo celebrations, Chinese New Year, Black History Month, an Asian festival, or Global Earth Day. You will not only meet new and different individuals from a variety of ethnic backgrounds, you will also learn firsthand about their cultures.

45. Choose a country to study and make a weekly date to learn more about it with your family, especially if you have children. Find out what foods the people eat and how they celebrate holidays. Learn phrases like "hello," "I love you," or "I need to use bathroom" in the language of that country.

46. Get your passport—and travel. Unfortunately, only 34 percent of Americans own passports. Learning about another culture from printed material, the Internet, or television is one thing, but immersing yourself in another culture leaves an impression that will stay with you the rest of your life.

47. Spend time observing the interactions of children. When my daughter was younger, I was always amazed at how easy it was for her to interact and develop instant friendships. When she met someone at a social gathering or play date, the two instantly connected. No shields, no barriers, no stereotypes. They simply enjoyed each other's company. Take time with your

children, nieces and nephews, or volunteer organizations and faith-based groups for kids to see how simple opening up to people who are different from you can be.

48. Spend one day in a wheelchair. Navigate it in a shopping center or another public place. Try bouncing a basketball or hitting a golf or tennis ball. For one day, put yourself in the shoes of someone who relies on a wheelchair for transportation and record your experience.

49. Choose a restaurant that features an authentic ethnic cuisine you've never experienced the next time you go out to dinner.

50. Volunteer at a senior center or Goodwill and record what you learned during your time there.

Additional Readings

DIVERSITY

The following vignettes were developed to facilitate a discussion on several diversity issues: gender, race, disability, age, religion, culture, and ethnicity. In reading these vignettes, please keep the following questions in mind:

1. Who is affected?
2. What are the likely consequences?
3. Are there any rights or duties at stake?
4. What principles are involved?
5. What are the implications for the characters in each vignette?

These vignettes have been developed from several sources. Some of them are fictionalized accounts of actual situations that have been reported in public sources. Others are disguised accounts based on the personal experiences of a number of students at MBA and executive programs from around the world who wish to remain anonymous. Finally, the vignettes reflect the general business experiences of the authors. All the vignettes are presented to facilitate class discussion rather than to illustrate the effective or ineffective handling of a business situation. Any resemblance to actual companies or people is entirely coincidental.

AT BAT

José Javier had been a senior consultant for an Indian software company for the past eight months. The transition to a foreign country had been difficult at first, and Javier, aware that in certain Indian communities there was little interaction among members of different ethnic groups, wondered how he would fit in. However, he had begun to enjoy New Delhi's hustle and bustle, which at times reminded him of his native Brasilia. His yearnings for *churrasco* and football had sparked an appetite for *dhosas* and an interest in cricket. Raafat al-Arabi, a friendly co-worker, had recently invited Javier to participate in a company cricket match. Javier was looking forward to playing cricket for the first time.

While awaiting his turn at bat, Javier overheard the Hindu CFO of the company make racist comments about the Muslim players on the team—including al-Arabi. Javier was a little surprised, since his experience over the past few months was that Hindus and Muslims seemed to work well together at the company, with little to no ethnic tension evident. Both groups had certainly been welcoming to him. Javier tried to put the remark out of his head as the cricket game continued and he focused on learning the rules.

After hearing the CFO's comments at the game, however, Javier began to pay closer attention to the ethnic undertones in the company. He noticed that only Hindus comprised the top management team. In a few discreet conversations with some of his Muslim co-workers, Javier realized that they did indeed encounter a glass ceiling when it came to promotion.

Several weeks later, Javier was in a meeting with the top management team when the CFO blamed recent earnings drops on the unreliability of Muslim workers. What should Javier do?

TO ACT OR NOT TO ACT?

John Davis was vice president of marketing at an established financial institution in New York City. He had just heard that the company's 2001 annual retreat was going to be held at a conference center set in the quiet South Carolina countryside. The location would be breathtaking except for one detail: The conference center had been a cotton plantation owned by a slaveholder in antebellum America.

Davis had grown up in the area and knew the conference center's historical significance. Since three of his upper-level managers were people of color, he wondered if he should talk to them and see if they would be as disturbed as he was about holding the retreat there. If his colleagues were not concerned, should he take action alone? Should he talk to the CEO to ask to have the locale changed or the event cancelled?

THE RESTAURANT BUSINESS

John Hansen was the manager of Peppercorn, an extremely popular restaurant/bar in Manhattan that catered to young professionals. Ever since Hansen had hired the highly talented chef, Tom Barbour, nine months earlier, the restaurant had experienced a surge of popularity. Although only 30 years old, Barbour was by far the best chef Hansen had ever worked with, and he had an engaging personality that both customers and employees loved.

A day earlier, one of Hansen's most trusted employees had revealed disturbing confidential information: Barbour was HIV-positive. Hansen had several concerns. Although his employees were careful and cautious in the kitchen, there was always the chance of an accident. Rarely did a month go by when one of his employees didn't cut or nick him- or herself with a knife, grater, or other utensil. What if Barbour had an accident? Hansen also worried about the reactions of his 14 employees *and* his customers should they find out about Barbour's condition. Would the news affect Hansen's restaurant business? What obligation did he have to Barbour, his employees, and the customers?

HIRING CHOICES

Betty Smith, head of human resources for the Widgetwise Company, had to hire a national sales manager. After many interviews, Smith had narrowed the field down to two candidates. Jack Taylor was clearly the top choice. He had finished first in his class at the prestigious Darden Business School, had great employment experience, and exceptional communication skills. The other candidate, Rita Manson, appeared to be capable and competent, but she lacked Taylor's fine credentials, proven track record, and engaging personality.

The problem? Jack Taylor was blind. Widgetwise, a public company, had a strong policy of hiring regardless of gender, race, religion, sexual orientation, or physical ability. But Smith realized that hiring Taylor posed several problems. Widgetwise would need to become "blind-friendly" so that Taylor and his seeing-eye dog could navigate the building. The company would need to install Braille signage, purchase Braille word-processing equipment, and hire additional secretarial help as well as a driver to aid Taylor in doing his job. Some senior managers were concerned that this investment—upfront and ongoing—would be hefty. They also worried that other employees might view the changes as favoritism.

Smith pondered additional concerns. How would customers react to negotiating with a blind sales manager who could not see the charts and graphs that were normally used in meetings? Would Taylor's presence require special training for the other employees? What about the potential legal liability if Taylor should trip and fall at work? What, if any, of the employees were allergic to—or even afraid of—dogs?

Nonetheless, Smith had to make a decision by the end of the day. What should that decision be?

DWB

Judy Wilson, entrepreneur and CEO of First Finished, Inc., was impressed by the symbolism of having just moved her business from downtown Detroit into the affluent Grosse Point suburb. Wilson and her manager of operations, Eric Gilbert, had spent most of the fall of 2001 looking for space that would accommodate the company's growth. The Grosse Point location seemed perfect. Wilson was excited about the transition, and the new office space offered a grand view.

Yet after only three months, Wilson felt a brewing problem needed to be addressed— Gilbert was continually arriving at the office late. He had been with First Finished since the company opened, and tardiness was just not one of Gilbert's traits. Because their relationship was based on a mutual respect that had grown into a friendship, Wilson decided to confront him. She asked Gilbert why, since the move, he was always late. His answer was simply, "DWB." In his explanation, Gilbert was very candid:

> Judy, I am a black man driving a white Mercedes from downtown Detroit into an affluent, predominately white suburban neighborhood. The police stop me no matter what route I take into this neighborhood. If I arrive on time it is because I wasn't stopped. But I refuse to cut short my morning ritual of coffee and the newspaper before I leave for work—to factor in the possibility that the police will hold me up for 15 minutes.

How should Wilson respond?

BIPOLAR DISORDER IN THE WORKPLACE

Bill Dodson, 52 and an engineer at Generationxtech, had bipolar disorder, which, for the most part, he had managed to control with medication and to conceal from his co-workers. Sometimes, however, his condition necessitated hospitalization, as it had recently when a severe manic episode resulted in a two-week hospital stay. His wife, Sheila, covered for him, telling his boss that Dodson had suffered a heart attack and dissuading any co-workers from visiting him.

Now out of the hospital, Dodson was about to return to work and was deliberating about whether to tell his boss the truth. His sister, Beth, who worked with the mentally ill, encouraged him to do so and reminded him that the Americans with Disabilities Act protected him from being fired. If the boss knew about Dodson's illness, Beth said, he could adjust to Dodson's illness and perhaps give him more flexibility at work. While Dodson welcomed flexibility, he knew there was still a great deal of prejudice about mental illness. He could not be fired, but he could be frozen out of assignments and kept from any responsibility, a situation Dodson knew he could not tolerate. At his age, however, it would be difficult to find a similar job at the same pay scale.

Should Dodson tell his boss the truth? Why or why not?

THE SCREEN SAVER

Ed Harrison owned and ran an ad agency with approximately 30 employees. Their offices were in a large converted warehouse with no individual offices, just cubicle dividers. This allowed for little privacy, but his staff, a close-knit and diverse group, did not seem to mind.

One afternoon, employee John Blank asked to speak with Harrison. Blank told Harrison that one of the accountants, a born-again Christian, had a "Christ is Risen" screensaver on his office computer and that, because he was a Jew, it bothered him as well as the 10 other Jewish employees. The accountant's desk was near the office entrance, and it was almost impossible not to see the screensaver as one entered. Blank had asked the employee once to change the screensaver, but the accountant had not, further angering the other Jewish employees.

What should Harrison do?

HIRING PRACTICES

Eric Loo has had a long career at Widget, Inc., the most successful company in all of Malaysia. Company founder Kiranjit Kaur had brought the new industry to the slowly developing democracy, in hopes of fostering prosperity. Most of Malaysia's economic growth was driven by export—particularly to China. Widget had brought much needed cash into the country and helped to finance education and agricultural initiatives. The company's emphasis on values and its record for excellent performance had made it a prime target for investors even a decade after Kaur's death.

The recent wave of global investors had made it possible for much-needed expansion in some departments. Loo's boss requested that he supervise the hiring of a new team member, with one stipulation: "Do you know any Chinese executives who would be interested in the job? We really need to make an effort to diversify the team, and I want our trading partners and investors to see how global we are." Loo was surprised, but he began interviewing candidates for the job. Many of them were not Malaysians.

After two weeks of interviews, Loo concluded that two people were the best candidates for the job, and both were Malaysian. Loo explained his recommendation to his boss, carefully presenting each candidate's background and abilities. Irritated, his boss said, "Wasn't I clear when I said we need a Chinese person in the group? We can't afford to be an all-Malaysian department. Besides, if it turns out the Chinese guy can't do the job we'll just move him to another department. What's the big deal?"

How should Loo respond? What are his options?

THE FRIDAY BLOWOUT

Angela Lopez was a senior engineer at Electrix, Inc. She worked closely with three other senior engineers. Two were quite mild-mannered, while the third—Steven Howell—was fairly aggressive in voicing his opinions. In a staff meeting one Friday morning, with both top and middle management present, Lopez and Howell openly disagreed about the details of one of the company's biggest current projects.

Later that day, Lopez's boss called her into his office. "I need you to try to tone it down in these meetings," he said. "It upsets the staff when you get so fiery." Lopez was stunned; she believed that "fiery" was a thinly veiled reference to her Latino heritage. She also knew that Howell was just as vociferous—if not more so—as she was in these meetings.

"Did you talk to Steven?" Lopez asked.

"No—we think the problem lies more with you" was the answer.

How should Lopez respond?

TASTY COLA

Gerry Nelson, director of marketing at Tasty Cola, was uneasy with her boss's suggestion that the company create an ethnic marketing committee to study methods of targeting different ethnic groups. The statistics were indisputable. While the average Caucasian consumer drank 130 liters of Tasty Cola a year, Mexican-Americans and African Americans averaged fewer than 50.

Nelson struggled with the concept of ethnic marketing. Because soft drinks fulfilled no basic human need, marketing them necessitated creating an emotional link between the product and the consumer. She was uncomfortable with tying emotion to ethnicity in Tasty Cola ads. How could the company attract one ethnic group without offending another? What were the ethical implications of essentially stereotyping ethnicities? How could Tasty Cola avoid ethnic stereotyping? Was there such thing as a positive stereotype?

DIVERSITY = DOLLARS

Companies that recruit, retain and reward a more diverse workforce are more profitable. Now it's time for latin american corporations to catch up.

— *CEDRIC HERRING*

For many people, gender diversity is important because it removes barriers that have historically prevented women from taking their rightful places in the corridors of power. But there's also a specific business case to be made: including more women in the corporate setting will help meet customers' needs, enrich understanding of the pulse of the marketplace and improve the quality of products and services.

The business case rests on what should be an obvious point: companies cannot effectively sell to women if they do not understand and value women, whether as customers or as employees. Therefore, increasing gender diversity in Latin American companies, especially in mass consumer-oriented sectors where women form large portions of the actual or potential customer base, will help boost their bottom line.

In the United States, proponents of diversity commonly make the claim that diversity pays. The greater the diversity among employees, the broader their perspectives, resulting in an ability to marshal a wider array of intellectual and cultural resources to solve problems. Diversity also is a source of creative conflict that can lead to a re-examination of assumptions that would otherwise be dominated by male points of view. The putative competitive advantages—fresh ideas, positive outreach and communication with customers, more qualified workers—have persuaded many companies that diversity can produce greater profits.

HOW IT WORKS

These claims about gender diversity and business outcomes are well-supported in the United States. For example, using a random sample of business organizations, a 2009 study showed that higher average sales revenues are associated with higher levels of gender diversity. The study revealed that the average revenues of businesses with low levels of gender diversity were roughly $45.2 million, compared with $299.4 million for those with medium levels of gender diversity, and $644.3 million for businesses with high levels of gender diversity. [see figure below]

Higher levels of gender diversity were also associated with greater numbers of customers.

The average number of customers for businesses with low levels of gender diversity was 20,500, compared to 27,100 for those with medium levels, and 36,100 for businesses with high levels. The analysis also showed that 62 percent of businesses with high levels of gender diversity reported higher than average market share, compared with 45 percent of those with low levels of gender diversity and 58 percent of businesses with medium levels of gender diversity.

The same was true in terms of reporting higher than average profitability. Fewer than half—45 percent—of businesses with low levels of gender diversity reported higher than average profitability. This compares with 62 percent of establishments with high levels of gender diversity and 58 percent

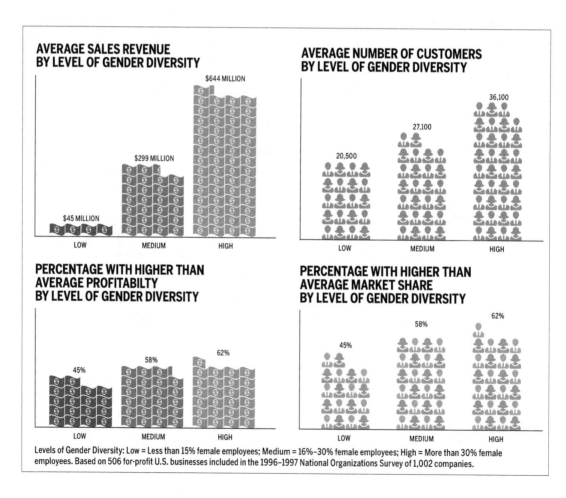

of those with medium levels of gender diversity. While studies documenting the link between gender diversity and business outcomes in Latin America are not as prevalent, there is little reason to believe that these patterns differ from the United States.

HOW THE LATIN AMERICAN PRIVATE SECTOR IS BEHIND AND WHAT CAN BE DONE ABOUT IT

Latin American companies lag behind North American and European companies in the area of gender diversity. Although increasing numbers of women in Latin America work in management jobs, they continue to confront glass ceilings. Latin American women constitute 10 percent of corporate presidents or vice presidents. Women hold less than 7 percent of companies' board seats in Mexico, 5 percent in Brazil, 7 percent in Argentina, 7 percent in Venezuela, and less than 2 percent in Chile. In contrast, women hold more than 16 percent of the corporate board positions in the U.S, and 73 percent of Fortune 500 companies in the U.S. have at least one female executive officer.

By increasing their focus on gender diversity, and by implementing the kinds of pro-women policies and programs that are becoming commonplace in other parts of the world, Latin American companies could reap great benefits. But a number of steps must be taken, by governments as well as companies.

First, while there have been steady improvements in the quantity of education—such as expanded enrollment and more years of schooling—there are gaps in the type of education available for women. Latin American governments can join in public-private partnerships to train women so their skills better match the needs of the market.

A good example is WE Americas (Women's Entrepreneurship in the Americas)—a recently launched public-private partnership to increase women's economic participation and to remove barriers women face when starting and growing businesses. The goal is to provide support to women entrepreneurs throughout Latin America and the Caribbean, expand women-led initiatives, and improve women's access to credit and other financial services." Such an initiative can help give companies a competitive advantage in the global market as well.

A second goal should be to promote gender equality in political participation. This can be accomplished by undertaking electoral reforms and making political parties more inclusive. For example, by encouraging parties to include an equitable number of female candidates in their slates, governments can also allocate resources and information to facilitate greater participation by women in the political process—and, in turn, greater attention to gender equality in public policies.

A third strategy for catalyzing the effects of gender diversity is to enact gender equity policies for the workplace, including for recruitment and retention. Offering job training opportunities for women

GENDER EQUALITY

What are Corporations Doing to Promote Diversity Internally?

BY WILDA ESCARFULLER

Women made up 46.6 percent of the U.S. labor force in 2011, but they came up short in the upper reaches of corporate governance. Only 14.1 percent of executive officer positions in Fortune 500 companies are held by women, according to the 2011 Catalyst Census—despite studies that have documented the economic case for gender equality at all levels of business.

Are corporations using model mechanisms to promote their female talent? Yes—but not enough. A 2010 ranking by Calvert Investments of Standard & Poor's 100 Index (S&P 100) companies by their diversity practices finds that, despite professed commitment to diversity, companies are reluctant to disclose diversity data—making it difficult to get a clear, accurate picture.

Companies receive a score of 0–100 based on presence (and disclosure) of an equal employment opportunity (EEO) policy; internal and external diversity initiatives; family-friendly benefits; the presence of women among executives and board members; director selection criteria; and overall corporate commitment.

Although no company scored zero, companies' transparency on every aspect was spotty. For example, though 74 percent of the companies surveyed support EEO guidelines about greater inclusiveness, only 8 percent fully disclosed the breakdown of their workforce by race and gender across employment categories.

Five companies scored at or above 95 on the Calvert scale. Citigroup Inc., which topped the list with 100 points, provides full EEO disclosure, while JPMorgan (95 points) offers many work-life benefits, including onsite childcare, adoption assistance, paternity leave, lactation programs, and domestic partner benefits. Chevron, another top performer, ties managers' performance ratings to their hiring of diverse candidates.

The major accountancy firms have also been leaders in workplace diversity: Pricewaterhouse Coopers (PwC) is recognized for its diversity at the CEO level, cross-cultural mentoring programs, expansive employee benefits, and use of resource groups in recruitment and talent development. Similarly, Deloitte & Touche has been held up as an example for its emphasis on mentorship, retention and promotion of minorities; 43 percent of its leadership (board of directors, U.S-based senior executives and business unit CEOs) are women or minorities.

and encouraging them to keep their skills current so that they can advance appears to pay dividends. Companies that offer formal job training are more diverse than those that do not; those that proactively select women for job training rather than let employees self-select are also more diverse. And those that offer family-friendly policies have the opportunity to do even better.

Also, employers can take advantage of transparency. Those that do things as simple as posting information about job vacancies and making use of internal hiring strategies (and presumably promote women from within) are more gender diverse. These strategies are consistent with the idea that organizations that foster woman-friendly climates have more success in retaining them. Many of these recruitment and retention efforts go hand in hand with signaling the importance of fairness in employment practices and providing job benefits that make it easier for companies to be inclusive.

Caterpillar, the U.S.-based maker of agricultural machinery, illustrates the point. Historically, Caterpillar was a laggard in terms of gender diversity. But after the 1980s, when it came close to bankruptcy, it stepped up its recruitment of women. By 2004, the company reported record-breaking profits and sales.

However, the company's diversity policies were not universally welcomed by its own employees. Male workers complained that women were getting promoted above men into management. In response, an internal educational program was established to promote greater understanding of company goals and practices. In 2006, Caterpillar also created the Women's Initiatives Network (WIN) to promote cultural awareness, mentoring, employee recruitment and retention, career development and community outreach—which increased support for its diversity programs.

By 2009, Caterpillar was ranked number 44 in the Fortune 500, and since 2010 the company has consistently been named one of the "Top 50 Employers" by *Woman Engineer* magazine. It has worked in Latin America as well. In 2011, Caterpillar-Brazil was recognized by *HSM* magazine as one of the "Top 50 Best Places to Work For" in Latin America.

Caterpillar also illustrates the fourth and final point. Companies must develop strategies to overcome the often stiff internal resistance to broadening diversity practices. Effective management of such disputes is important if companies want to reap the full benefits of bringing more women into their workplaces.

Governments in Latin America can respond to low levels of gender diversity by encouraging more of it, discouraging it, or ignoring it. Those working through such processes must be willing to confront the hard issues, and will need to recognize the distinct historical and cultural experiences that have set different paths for men and women in different countries. Today, reaping higher profits and competing with the rest of the world means that companies, and the countries in which they are based, must abandon policies that have stunted their growth and potential.

EXPANDING MULTICULTURAL EDUCATION TO INCLUDE FAMILY DIVERSITY

— TAMMY A. TURNER-VORBECK

INTRODUCTION

The composition of families is changing (Huston, 2001) and is readily apparent in the variety of families represented by students in today's classrooms. Advocates from the fields of social work and psychological counseling (Okun, 1996) as well as from adoptive, step, and gay family support networks (Geis-Rockwood, 1990) have come to the fore to call for changes in curriculum and for teacher education programs to recognize and address this often-neglected form of diversity; yet, the multicultural education and diversity issues discussed in today's teacher education courses at our major universities and colleges are often still restricted to their foundational concerns with discussions of race, ethnicity, class, and gender.

Introducing the topic of family diversity provides another dimension of diversity for preservice teachers to consider and explore while they try to construct meanings for the monumental topics under discussion and critique in teacher education classrooms. The very notion of "family" offers most students some degree of ownership in the topic through their personal experiences of family; however, as they are asked to deconstruct narrow societal definitions of what constitutes a family, they begin a journey that often leads to discomfort, resistance, and challenges to what is defined as a normal and valued family in our society.

The contentiousness of this sort of conversation mirrors and buttresses issues surrounding race, class, and gender across their multicultural education curriculum, but the topic of family allows uniquely personal access to powerful stereotypes and biases hidden deep within each student's conceptions of what constitutes a family.

This article describes a research and teaching project that was designed and implemented to investigate the promise of the integration of family diversity issues into a preservice teacher multicultural education curriculum to better prepare preservice teachers to respond to the needs of all students, regardless of their varied familial backgrounds.

RATIONALE

The overall purpose of this research project was to investigate the promise of the exploration of family diversity issues through a multicultural education curriculum to heighten the awareness and sensitivity of preservice teachers to needs tied to students' differing family structures as well as to overall issues of diversity in the classroom in order to better prepare these teachers to meet the needs of an increasingly diverse student population. Preservice teachers were introduced to family diversity issues as a special unit of instruction placed inside the existing curriculum in the undergraduate multicultural education course at a major Midwestern university's teacher education program. This research continues as part of an ongoing research project investigating how family diversity is addressed in both teacher education programs and multicultural education as a whole, including both theory and practice.

Issues of family diversity are becoming of critical importance as the demographics of families in this country and, indeed, the world, change (Huston, 2001); yet they are often an ignored part of the broader diversity discussions. Through the investigation of this project, participant awareness of family diversity issues was identified and assessed in terms of participant willingness to recognize and address such issues in their own classrooms. In addition, it is believed that providing these preservice teachers with opportunities to explore issues of diversity through the specific subject area of family structure holds the potential to heighten their overall sensitivity to the broader diversity issues of class, race, ethnicity, and language and to further struggle to avoid generalizations which sometimes accompany such concepts, generalizations that have often either become loaded with preconceived connotations or reduced to complete ambiguity as simply "multicultural" (Derman-Sparks, 1989).

There is little doubt that there exists a broad call for the inclusion of diversity issues throughout teacher education discussions. Much of this discussion takes place under the umbrella of multicultural studies. Scholars writing in the area of multiculturalism today emphasize the need for pervasive antiracist education aimed at social justice (Nieto, 2000), suggest content integration, knowledge construction, prejudice reduction, equity pedagogy, and the creation of an empowering school culture (Banks & Banks, 2001), argue for a *cultivation of humanity* (Nussbaum, 1997), call for *culturally responsive teaching*

(Gay, 2000), and attempt to define genres of multiculturalism, each with their own definitions and goals (Bennett, 2001; Duarte & Smith, 2000).

In preservice teacher university classrooms all over this country, future educators are engaged in attempts to make meaning of these notions and imagine their application to real students in real classrooms. With areas such as race and ethnicity forming the foundation of these studies, there also exists a need for an examination of other aspects of diversity which represent the varied physical and social worlds within which today's schoolchildren live and learn and family diversity represents a very important one.

MODES OF INQUIRY

This writing illustrates the work done and insights gained in this ongoing research effort. Phase one of this project involved the completion of a literature review of relevant writings in the areas of family diversity and curriculum and educational practices in the classroom. Building upon what was learned in phase one, phase two involved the design and creation of a unit of instruction tailored to both meet the needs of a preservice teacher audience and to also provide for analysis of preservice teachers' attitudes toward non-traditional families and children from those families as well as their abilities and willingness to work collaboratively to identify personal prejudices and how those might translate into the classroom.

The participants were preservice teachers (predominantly White, European-American) within the teacher education program of a prominent Midwestern university which offers a reformed teacher education program redesigned in terms of research findings on best practices. This teacher education program includes a focus on traditional diversity topics such as race, gender, culture, and language issues.

The family diversity curriculum unit was introduced to a total of three sections of the single, required Multicultural Education course within the teacher education curriculum across three semesters. Each section contained an average of twenty-six students. A summated, five-point Likert scale questionnaire provided foundational data on student attitudes toward family diversity and curriculum issues (Miller, 1991) as well as a focal point for reflection when returned to participants during their journal writing activities at the conclusion of the lesson. A less formal survey discussion at the end of the lesson provided formative feedback on the success of the lesson overall (Smith & Ragan, 1993).

In addition, guided discussions where the participants were encouraged to actively encounter and answer questions of their own prejudices and belief systems provided a strong foundation for self-exploration which was also reflected upon and evident during the journaling experience

(Clandinin & Connelly, 1994) as well as integrated into the activities. The guided group activities included the construction of a K-5 classroom activity for a lesson on family. Such activities created an opportunity for the participants to bring to life anti-bias activities involving family diversity which could be used in their own future classrooms. All of these activities were also reflected upon in the journal writing activity.

THE FAMILY DIVERSITY CURRICULUM UNIT

Syllabus space and time are both very precious within a multicultural education course designed to function as the only class within a reformed teacher education program dedicated to addressing issues of diversity and equity. As such, the addition of this curriculum unit on the topic of family diversity was allotted two hours of class time. During the class session before the Family Diversity Unit, a brief introduction to the upcoming unit was provided, the attitudinal questionnaires were administered and collected (anonymity was maintained), and the short, foundational readings were assigned and provided (*Understanding Diverse Families* and *Anti-bias Curriculum*; see references). The Family Diversity Unit was then taught during the next class period. A description of the curriculum unit is provided in the space that follows.

LAYING THE FOUNDATION

After spending a few minutes on introductions, the overarching research question for the project was shared with students as a point of orientation: "How can teachers help their classrooms to become more inclusive and accepting environments for children from differing family structures just as we know they should be sensitive to the gender, racial, cultural, and language differences of students?" The opening query uniformly resulted in a majority of students admitting that they had not previously considered that family diversity would be a likely issue in their classrooms or in their curricula.

Following the brief discussion of the introduction of the topic of family diversity, the objectives for the unit were openly shared with students: (1) Develop an awareness and an initial understanding of the issue of family diversity, (2) Discover our own opinions and biases on family diversity, (3) Create/explore some tools for use in the classroom, and (4) Reflect on our views of family diversity through journaling.

OBJECTIVE 1: DEVELOP AWARENESS AND INITIAL UNDERSTANDING OF FAMILY DIVERSITY

To accomplish the first objective of developing an initial understanding of the topic, a very brief lecture was given to provide foundational information. The changing demographics of our nation's school population were addressed, including the fact that less than fifty percent of children in schools in America are represented by a two biological, heterosexual parent family and that the trend away from traditional, nuclear families is increasing. This demonstrates the necessity for teachers to contemplate how they will address and work with issues of family diversity in their classrooms.

A few short narratives, collected from people from non-traditional families, in which they shared some of their personal painful school experiences were read to the students to help to put a human face on the real consequences of teacher ignorance or indifference toward family diversity. Various forms of families were introduced (e.g., foster, adopted, step, grandparent/relative, gay/lesbian, interracial, etc.) to expose students to a wide variety of forms of family with which they might not have been familiar.

To compliment descriptions of difference, a discussion of the unifying themes across families was provided. This notion is based upon how families function with similar goals and purposes such as "providing for basic needs, child rearing, socializing members, establishing and maintaining cultural traditions, and delegating responsibilities and roles."

OBJECTIVE 2: DISCOVER STUDENT OPINIONS AND BIASES ON FAMILY DIVERSITY

The second objective was achieved through a guided discussion of the two assigned readings as well as discovery of the students' own biases. The students were asked to write down their responses to this question: "Being honest, what are some of the personal prejudices you hold or have previously held about non-traditional (single-parent, adoptive, gay/lesbian, stepparent, multi-racial, etc.) families?"

Students were then asked to move into pairs to share their responses with a partner and to work together to complete these two questions: "How do you think those prejudices translate into the classroom environment?" and "How, as a teacher, might you create a more positive, accepting environment for children from non-traditional families?"

The class was reconvened as a whole group and answers to the question of biases held about differing forms of family were verbally volunteered, written on the board, and discussed. Responses to the second group of questions answered in pairs were then collected and discussed. Many students were amazed at the extent to which they and their classmates held strong prejudicial beliefs against non-traditional forms of family.

OBJECTIVE 3: CREATE ACTIVITIES FOR USE IN THE CLASSROOM ON FAMILY DIVERSITY

Having laid a foundational understanding of family diversity, followed by guided discovery of existing biases held by students, the third objective provided a positive and practical direction in which to turn by requiring some creative thinking about how to use classroom activities to be inclusive of many forms of family.

The exercise began by first critiquing the traditional family activities where seemingly innocuous assignments were exposed as having a negative impact on many children. Students from non-traditional family structures often feel awkward and excluded when asked to write an autobiography, bring baby photos to class, make a family tree, or doing genealogy studies. If they are being raised by single parents, step-families, grandparents/relatives, gay parents, or in adoptive or foster families, they will likely have some background that is missing, complicated, or even kept secret. Well meaning teachers can be exclusionary by using such familiar activities without realizing it.

An example of an inclusive alternative to the traditional activities, called the ME Poem, was shared with the class. In this activity, students are encouraged to complete each of nine descriptive statements about themselves, their interests, and their lives, including family members:

1. MOLLY (first name)
2. smart, athletic, funny, crazy (4 adjectives)
3. sister of Maureen (family)
4. who loves Mom, Maureen, Dad, and Judy
5. who needs love, good friends, and loyalty
6. who wonders about other cultures, diseases, and other states
7. who would like to see Florida, Paris, and people being nice to everyone else
8. resident of Petaluma, California, on Ellis Street
9. REGIN (last name)

The class was then instructed to break into small groups of three or four students and work with the markers and large sheets of paper provided to create a unique activity which could allow K-5 students to express information about themselves and their families in a free and unrestricted fashion. The excitement in the room surrounding this exercise was always palpable and the ideas generated were enthusiastically shared in a lively "show and tell" session afterward. Students routinely expressed satisfaction with their ability to ideate a tangible solution to the challenge of using inclusive activities on family. Additional commercially available examples of such activities, materials, and lessons were then provided, such as the film and accompanying instructor's guide, *That's a Family!*.

OBJECTIVE 4: REFLECT ON VIEWS OF FAMILY DIVERSITY THROUGH JOURNALING

Before giving students their reflective journaling assignment to be completed outside of class, the overall class totals for the attitudinal questionnaire were shared (maintaining individual confidentiality). Their individual completed questionnaires were then returned to them by use of a special labeling code. The journaling assignment sheet with the following questions was then given out:

Use your own paper and thoughtfully answer the questions that follow. This should represent approximately 2 to 3 pages of written reflection. Return your assignment to your instructor.

- Thinking back over the readings on family diversity, what issue(s) intrigued you most or caused you to think about something you had not considered before?

- During the class discussions, many issues concerning family diversity surfaced. What made the biggest impression on you and why?
- How do you feel that these issues have impacted your ideas about teaching?
- Do you see any of these ideas translating into your own teaching practice? How?
- Do you have any personal experiences which you can relate to this discussion?

Revisit the answers you gave on the questionnaire. How would you answer these questions now?

- Describe what FAMILY DIVERSITY means to you.
- What types of families do you expect to see represented by the students you will teach?

FINDINGS

In the course of participating in this project, participants were exposed to readings on family diversity written from the perspectives of people living these experiences. Bringing these family situations to life was an important part of the experience, overall. Through the attitudinal questionnaire and subsequent discussions, participants were asked to search into their own histories and to explore their own biases against particular family structures and how they thought those biases might or might not impact upon their teaching.

In addition to discussing the affective elements involved in the teaching of students from non-traditional families, participants were also able to "deconstruct" traditional classroom activities on the topic of family, often thought of nostalgically (such as the "family tree" activity) but shown to be detrimental to children who have hidden histories or simply lack that information altogether. Participants were then able to work together in small groups to create new and innovative activities that would be inclusive of all students.

Tying this all together and mirroring the theory-into-practice notion, participants reflected again upon their original answers to the questionnaire on attitudes toward differing family structures, their experiential readings and discussions, traditional exclusionary activities and improvements upon those, and their new perspectives on family diversity and how to address it in the classroom environment.

ATTITUDINAL QUESTIONNAIRE

The attitudinal questionnaire consisted of ten Likert-type questions and two open-ended questions. It was designed to provide a baseline for locating the beliefs about families held by each participant and for participant reflection upon their responses after the unit's completion. The closed-ended questions asked for degrees of agreement or disagreement (5 = Strongly Agree, 4 = Agree, 3 = Undecided, 2 = Disagree, 1 = Strongly Disagree) and the results are provided below.

Question 1

As a teacher, you would worry about children in your class whose parents were divorced. (64% Agreed or Strongly Agreed)

Question 2

The definition of a family is a group of people in which there are two married, biological parents who are both living at home and caring for their children. (16% Agreed or Strongly Agreed)

Question 3

You plan to use a "family tree" exercise to talk about family genealogy and help children to be proud of their "roots." (68% Agreed or Strongly Agreed)

Question 4

Talking openly in the classroom about gay and/or lesbian relationships is a form of supporting those types of relationships. (12% Agreed or Strongly Agreed)

Question 5

You plan to hold a "Bring your grandparents to school day." (64% Agreed or Strongly Agreed)

Question 6

You feel sorry for the children of single mothers because they do not receive the amount of attention and support they need at home to be successful at school. (36% Agreed or Strongly Agreed)

Question 7

Not mentioning types of families other than traditional, two-parent families can cause a student from a non-traditional family to suffer self-esteem troubles. (63% Agreed or Strongly Agreed)

Question 8

You plan to practice an anti-bias curriculum. (68% Agreed or Strongly Agreed)

Question 9

You often think to yourself, "Why can't we just let children be?" or "Children don't have any prejudices." (16% Agreed or Strongly Agreed)

Question 10

Children who were adopted are no different than other children in terms of their development and their needs at school. (60% Agreed or Strongly Agreed)

The open-ended questions produced a variety of responses as participants were asked to consider: (1) *Describe what family diversity means to you*, and (2) *What types of families do you expect to see represented by the students you will teach?* Some students revealed inclusive definitions of families that went beyond the traditional, nuclear family. A larger number demonstrated an understanding that a significant number of the students in their future classrooms would not be from traditional, nuclear family structures. Overall, the results of the attitudinal questionnaire indicated and provided some illumination of the biases that existed prior to the family diversity unit.

REFLECTIVE JOURNALS

Since time spent with the students was limited, it was from the reflective journals data that evidence of growth among participants became apparent. Below are three excerpts from student participant reflective journals:

"SUSAN"

The biggest impression made on me was what my fellow classmates seemed to think about family diversity. Some of them seemed quick to judge others simply on what choices they had made. I think this attitude may impair them when it comes to teaching kids because it is hard to judge parents and not judge their children as well. My religion tells me not to believe in homosexuality but after discussing these issues in this unit, I also believe that you cannot judge children negatively because you personally disagree with decisions their parents have made. I want to make all of the kids in my class feel like they belong.

"JOY"

Family diversity is a concept that was never previously discussed during my education. Our class discussion really made me think about it. I cannot understand how in one sentence a person can say that a child needs two loving parents in a home and then also go on to say that homosexual parents cannot provide that. This issue has really opened my mind and eyes personally and also in thinking about how to handle such the topic of "different" families when I become a teacher myself.

"SARAH"

What made the biggest impression on me was when we listed our biases on the board. I felt so over-whelmed by these biases. I know that I am guilty of having some of these negative thoughts but I hadn't even realized before that I even held them. I don't know exactly how to remove these biases but the unit on family diversity has gotten my attention and I will take some of these new ideas with me when I teach. I now think it is important for me to remember to be as aware as possible of the backgrounds of all of my students and to also be aware of my own biases toward those backgrounds.

IMPLICATIONS

Overall, this research project indicates that expanding the definition and scope of multicultural educa-tion curriculum holds the potential to prepare new teachers to practice diverse family inclusion in several ways: (1) by broadening preservice teacher awareness of diversity to include family structure diversity since the composition of the American family has changed drastically and continues to evolve, (2) by assisting preservice teachers in discovering and examining their own prejudices concerning children from diverse family backgrounds and providing them with ways to address those biases, and (3) by exposing pre-service teachers to ways to reflect upon their own thoughts and practices as well as ways to work collaboratively with others to raise awareness and solve problems.

Additionally, as a teacher educator and a mother of three children adopted at older ages from the state foster care system, I find the necessity of empowering teachers to confidently and proactively address family diversity in curriculum and in the classroom to be of critical importance. Curricular conceptual representations of family must be reshaped to accurately reflect and honor the many and varied ways in which people form caring groups that support and honor their members. Curriculum, widely conceived, refers to both formal forms of curriculum such as lessons, textbooks, and activities as well as informal forms of curriculum such as school culture (teacher speech, school functions, and paperwork) and popular culture (movies, television, and books).

Teachers need to be made aware that commercially-prepared lessons and textbook depictions of families and family life remain today still focused upon a traditional, nuclear family with a few ethnic variations of this theme presented in the more progressive versions. These limited depictions of family represent a standard of family against which we are all to measure our own.

Perhaps less obvious are aspects of school culture which contribute to a lack of inclusiveness of varied forms of family. School paperwork forms that are sent home with students to be completed by adults at home are still designed to identify and designate a responsible parent and are usually not flexible enough to allow for the accurate reflection of the complex caretaking networks formed by many current family conditions.

Classroom assistance is still most often sought under the moniker of "Room Mothers." Teacher talk about concerns for children from single parent (read: dysfunctional) homes is rampant and thinly disguised, if at all. Parents are sometimes even directly subjected to teacher prejudice on the psychological soundness of family forms with remarks given such as "I'll be watching for abandonment issues to surface in your child" when the child is identified as adopted. In conservative climates, even in public (as opposed to parochial) schools, students are openly but off-the-record told that a gay, lesbian, and/or transgender lifestyle is immoral (Turner-Vorbeck, 2005).

Mimicking the narrow and limited images of family portrayed through formal curriculum and school culture are those created and perpetuated through mass media and popular culture. Informal curriculum in the form of popular culture has become heavily influential due to the amount of exposure students receive to various forms of media such as movies, television, and books and it serves to buttress what students are learning about families in schools. Most popular, top-selling children's books and related television series and movies such as the *Berenstain Bears* books (Berenstain & Berenstain, 1962), the *Arthur* books (Brown, 1976), the *American Girl* doll stories (Tripp, 1991) and even the *Harry Potter* books (Rowling, 1997) continue to feature portrayals of families in the literary and visual images of American child culture that still consist largely of traditional, two parent households with the mother fulfilling the role of primary nurturer and caregiver (Turner-Vorbeck, 2005).

As discussed here, limited attempts on the part of classroom materials and textbook publishers to broaden conceptions and discussions of family, damaging talk, procedures, policies, and negative biases largely held and commonly practiced in school culture, and the predominance of traditional images and portrayals of exclusively nuclear family forms in curriculum and popular culture should leave teachers and parents alarmed at the chronic incongruence of the curricular representations of family to the actual, living, everyday families of our students. Yet, there still exists the possibility of representations and discussions of family becoming more inclusive through continued research, education, and dialogue such as that presented in this special edition of *Multicultural Education*.

REFERENCES

Banks, J. & Banks, C. (2001). *Multicultural education: Issues & perspectives* (4th ed.). New York: Wiley.

Bennett, C. (2001). Genres of research in multicultural education. *Review of Educational Research, 71* (2), pp.171–217.

Berenstain, S. & Berenstain, J. (1962). *The big honey hunt.* New York: Beginner Books

Brown, M. (1976). *Arthur's nose.* Boston: Little, Brown & Company.

Clandinin, D. & Connelly, F. (1994). Personal experience methods. In N.K. Denzin & Y.S. Lincoln (Eds.), *Handbook of qualitative research* (pp. 413–427). Thousand Oaks, CA: Sage.

Derman-Sparks, L. (1989). *Anti-bias curriculum.* Washington, DC: National Association of Education for Young Children.

Duarte, E. & Smith, S. (2000). *Foundational perspectives in multicultural education.* New York: Addison Wesley Longman.

Gay, G. (2000). *Culturally responsive teaching: Theory, research, & practice.* New York: Teachers College Press.

Geis-Rockwood, W. (1990). *Shapes: Families of today* (2nd edition). Santa Barbara, CA: Stepfamily Association of America.

Huston, P. (2001). *Families as we are: Conversations from around the world.* New York: The Feminist Press.

Miller, D. (1991). *Handbook of research design and social measurement* (5th edition). Newbury Park, CA: Sage.

Nieto, S. (2000). *Affirming diversity: The sociopolitical context of multicultural education* (3rd edition). New York: Longman.

Nussbaum, M. (1997). *Cultivating humanity.* Cambridge, MA: Harvard University Press.

Okun, B. (1996). *Understanding diverse families: What practitioners need to know.* New York: The Guilford Press.

Rowling, J. (1997). *Harry Potter and the sorcerer's stone.* New York: Scholastic Press.

Smith, P. & Ragan, T. (1993) *Instructional design.* Upper Saddle River, NJ: Prentice- Hall.

Tripp, V. (1991). *Meet Felicity.* Middleton, WI: Pleasant Company Publications.

Turner-Vorbeck, T. (2005). Representations of family in curriculum: A post-structural analysis. In C. Cherryholmes, E. Heilman, & A. Segall (Eds.), *Social studies—The next generation: Researching social studies in the postmodern.* New York: Peter Lang.

TRAINING ACROSS GENERATIONS

KIM A. ROWE

ENGAGING THE GENERATIONS

Close your eyes for a moment and think of a typical classroom from your school days—the smell of chalk or dry erase markers, the murmur of students as they ponder an assignment, the sight of the teacher handing out tests. Now open your eyes. Did you imagine a classroom where Jimmy was 60 years younger than his classmate, Jane? Were some of the students in their teens, while others were in their 30s or 50s or perhaps even 70s? Was the teacher more mature than the students, or was she several generations younger? These examples may seem outlandish, but they are actually reflective of the crazy quilt of generations in today's workplace.

As you look around your own company, you'll find

- **veterans**, born approximately between 1920 and 1945
- **baby boomers**, born approximately between 1946 and 1965
- **Generation X**, born approximately between 1966 and 1980
- **Generation Y**, born approximately between 1981 and 2000.

You may know that there are four distinct generations in the workplace. But did you know that while the different generations share many things, they have their own preferences for how they like to learn? Learning style preferences are driven largely by elementary school experience, but other shared cultural experiences influence how each generation learns best.

This *Infoline* provides insights to learning and development specialists who are faced with the challenge of designing and delivering learning opportunities for employees of all ages. This issue will show you

- learning preferences of the four generations in the workplace

- tips and techniques for enhancing learning for members of each generation
- strategies for training multiple generations at the same time.

WHO ARE THE GENERATIONS?

The majority of the oldest generation, the veterans, are long past the minimum retirement age. For the first time, however, many people are postponing retirement well into their 70s, with many individuals taking on second careers and extending their working lives. The veterans are soon to be joined by the baby boomers, who will retire in record numbers during the next 15 years, leaving behind a significant gap in corporate experience and knowledge that must be filled by the younger generations following them. By one conservative estimate, 46 million baby boomers are expected to leave the workforce by 2017.

Generation X is half as numerous as the baby boomers, but they are followed by a much larger group, Generation Y. As the baby boomers retire and more positions open up than there are Gen Xers to fill, Generation Y will have opportunities for promotion earlier in their careers and will require professional development opportunities to support their career growth.

...

The Importance of Learning

It is interesting to note that all the generations, from Generation Y to veterans, report that training opportunities play a role in keeping them at their companies. In 2000, a survey done by BridgeWorks, a consulting firm, found 48 percent of veteran generation workers said that training played a role in keeping them at the company; 45 percent of baby boomers and 58 percent of Gen Xers said the same thing. Generation Y, the most educated generation yet (64 percent of women and 60 percent of men go to college), was brought up by baby boomer parents who put a great deal of emphasis on education; so training in the workplace is important to them.

Deloitte, a professional services firm, published a study in 2007 that found Generation Y respondents rated development and training as the most valued incentives a company could offer. In the same study, they rated training equal in importance to salary.

...

LEARNING PREFERENCES

Individual members of a generation went to school at about the same time and were influenced by the teaching styles, curriculum, and values of the era. Members of a generation experienced similar classroom rules and expectations, and grew comfortable with the same types of technology (or lack thereof) in the classroom. They experienced the same cultural influences and major historical events that had an impact on the way they currently act, learn, and think. While not every member of a generation will behave the same way, a significant number of individuals in that generation share characteristics that have become hallmarks of the group.

Let's look of the four generations to see how their formative years influenced their learning preferences. It is relatively easy to understand why certain generations prefer learning in specific ways when you understand a little about their background.

Veterans

The veteran generation (also called *traditionalists*) is the oldest generation in the workplace. People born between 1920 and 1945 fall into this generation group.

Influential Events

The generation was highly influenced by what is arguably the most global of all formative events: World War II. These individuals saw their parents struggle through the Great Depression, and learned to live conservatively, stretch a dollar, and make do financially. The veterans were the original practitioners of the three Rs—Reduce, Reuse, Recycle—for fiscal reasons, not environmental.

When the veterans went to school (and not everyone had that luxury) they learned in classrooms where strict discipline and order were the rule; teachers held complete authority. Women in this age group became the first female workforce as they stepped in to handle the factory jobs deserted as the men enlisted to fight in WWII. They had faith in government and its leaders, and were proud of their identity as U.S. citizens and members of the U.S. military. After the war, people of this generation became the first to realize the American dream of a spouse, three kids, and a home of their own.

Members of the second half of this generation, born after 1930, were not old enough to serve in World War II, but many went on to serve in the Korean War. They are sometimes referred to as the Silent Generation, a term first used in *Time* magazine in 1951, because they never developed a strong generational identity of their own. Instead, they identified closely with the veterans before them, mimicking their values and preferences. The youngest of this group adopted many of the generational characteristics of the baby boomer generation that followed.

Impact on Learning

As a result of going through some tough financial times, when education was a luxury, many veterans are very appreciative of learning opportunities in the workplace. Many see training as evidence that management values their contribution to the success of the organization. Veterans' experiences as members of a massive military success as well as the expectations of cultural conformity that came in the post-war years have an effect on their personalities in the classroom. Veterans are likely to

- respect authority
- dislike informality
- appreciate consistency, logic, and discipline.

Their greatest comfort comes in being an anonymous part of the group. In training settings, try not to put them on the spot or force them to step out of their comfort zone too quickly.

For more, see the sidebar *Veteran Characteristics*.

Veteran Generation Training Tips

- Provide alternative scheduling and flexibility. Veterans are winding down their careers, and many are looking for ways to stay in the game and earn income while keeping time for health-care appointments, grandchildren, travel, and other retirement pursuits.
- Give them the message that they are respected and valued as part of the workforce. Make sure that members of the veteran generation can see themselves in all your training materials (video, interactive, print, and so on). Include them as training group leaders and mentors. Use appropriate and respectful language and forms of address. Ask if they would like your help before offering coaching or guidance.
- Design a comfortable training setting. Veterans may be experiencing health-related difficulties like stiffness from arthritis and compromised hearing and eyesight. Provide good lighting and comfortable chairs in the training areas.
- Test all your handouts and computer-based training to see if they are easily read by people with bifocals.
- Take lots of breaks to allow older workers to get up and stretch.
- Use classroom training settings when possible; this group enjoys presentations and lectures by topic experts. On-the-job training works well for veterans as long as stress and the potential for embarrassment are minimized, and the trainer is respectful and sensitive to their needs.
- Assume that veterans are technologically capable. While veterans may take longer to learn new skills, they are not technology averse.

THE CHANGING WORKPLACE

According to Claire Raines, a widely published author on the subject of generations, the challenge of educating multiple generations in a workplace learning center is a relatively recent phenomenon. Until the late 1980s, organizations maintained a hierarchy that kept mostly older people in more senior positions, while younger workers held staff roles. The training offered to these two groups was by default segregated by generation, with the youngest workers forming the majority of training class participants.

Today, a number of trends are changing the generational makeup of training classes. These factors all contribute to the changing workplace:

- Corporations are more likely to promote workers based on their talent rather than age, tenure, or experience.
- Older employees are continuing to work rather than retire, which brings individuals of more advanced age back into rank-and-file staff positions.
- Skill and knowledge gaps are being created by baby boomers who are leaving their jobs for retirement, forcing employers to offer creative solutions, including opportunities for training and education, to keep their older employees on the job.

The result? Training departments are struggling to adapt their onboarding curricula and management and leadership training programs to the needs of individuals of all ages.

VETERAN CHARACTERISTICS

Veteran Generation	
Formative Events	**Learning Preferences**
Economic hard times and boom years Awareness of how hard it can be leads to appreciation for education.	• Very grateful for learning opportunities. • See training as evidence of appreciation of their work.
World War II, Korean War, military service Faith in government and strong leadership; conformists were valued and individuals were proud to be part of a U.S. military unit.	• Like consistency, logic, discipline. • Dislike too much familiarity, overly casual dress or speech. • Respectful of authority—prefer trainer who is a credible authority figure. • Want respect from others in return.
The American dream Corporations valued loyalty, conformity, commitment to the company; everyone wanted a spouse, three kids, and a house with a picket fence.	• Want to remain an anonymous part of the group. • Do not want to be put on the spot. • Unlikely to confront facilitator.
Orderly classrooms Strong authority figures; children were "best seen but not heard"; corporal punishment common.	• Want organized, low-risk learning environment. • Prefer classroom-style room setup and trainer who follows established ground rules.

- Give them the opportunity to practice skills in private. Design transfer exercises in a way that allows the veteran learner to practice without embarrassment in front of other learners. Be careful not to call them out in front of the group or embarrass them in front of their peers.

Baby Boomers

The first generation to grow up with a television in the home; baby boomers were born between 1946 and 1965.

Influential Events

In 1966 this group was so influential that it appeared on the cover of *Time* magazine's Man of the Year issue. Baby boomers were the first generation to attend college in record numbers, and they became the most educated generation compared to any previous one in the United States.

They are projected to live longer than any previous generation, and grew up in an era when new scientific and medical advances were made every day. This was the era of the Beatles, Vietnam, resistance to the draft, bra-burning, Title IX, and marches on Washington.

Baby boomers are, for a variety of reasons, opting to work long past their traditional retirement age either by extending their years at their current company or by starting fresh with another organization.

BEWARE OF MYTHS

Generational research shows that there are common characteristics that bind together members of each generation. These characteristics include behaviors, traits, and learning preferences, and are the result of common events and cultural experiences that members of the generation shared during their formative years, that is, between birth and approximately the age of 18.

However, when working with individuals, don't assume that every generational characteristic will apply. Not every member of a given generation thinks alike, behaves alike, identifies with, or relates to others in that generation.

Beware of myths such as
- younger workers don't have much of a work ethic
- older workers are stuck in their ways.

Myths such as these can get you into trouble. Use the generational characteristics in this issue as a guideline, but always keep an open mind and avoid stereotyping.

Many are taking the opportunity to follow a dream, work for a not-for-profit organization, or start their own business.

Impact on Learning

As baby boomers enter new careers, they will make up a new, greyer demographic in the corporate training classroom. These older workers benefit from hands-on, application-focused techniques that help them internalize new information and skills.

Be aware of the pace in the classroom—if it is too fast, slow it down or give them an extra opportunity to put the new information into action before moving on.

Avoid an authoritarian style of teaching; baby boomers respond negatively toward it. Praise them often and point out the concrete benefits of the training.

For more, see the sidebar *Baby Boomer Characteristics.*

Baby Boomer Generation Training Tips

- Don't include managers in training sessions; baby boomers may feel they are being monitored or evaluated by their bosses.
- Treat boomers as equals, even if you are younger. Baby boomers do not want to feel like they are 20 years older than the instructor...even if they are.
- Don't come in as a heavy authority figure.
- Use storytelling and anecdotes to relate to boomers in a friendly, peer-to-peer fashion.
- Create a comfortable training environment that is safe for open discussion.
- Show baby boomers they are valued: Give feedback, offer thanks for efforts, learn their names, give them chances to talk, ask for their input, and refer to their experience.
- Create fair rules for all activities—according to generational learning expert, Julie Coates, boomers grew up in a very competitive environment, where some individuals lost and some won. It was OK to lose, as long as the rules were fair.
- Incorporate practical and fun activities that allow boomers to work in small groups or teams; use caution with role play, which might be fraught with too much potential for failure.
- Choose activities that don't put anyone on the spot or potentially expose weaknesses in front of others.

BABY BOOMER CHARACTERISTICS

Baby Boomer Generation	
Formative Events	**Learning Preferences**
Economic boom times Unprecedented, huge generation; entire infrastructure (schools, hospitals, and so on) developed to accommodate the number of boomers.	• Highly competitive. • Insist on fairness in competition. • Concerned with how they look to superiors and peers. • Believe that experience trumps education. • See themselves as forever young.
Civil rights, feminism, Vietnam Grass roots protests led the generation to believe they could can change the world.	• High achievers. • Workaholic approach to learning. • Willing to put in extra effort to achieve success. • May want an active role or voice in content and curriculum.
Beginning of the tech revolution	• Many use technology as the means, not the end.
Disappointment and disillusionment Kennedy assassinations; Martin Luther King Jr. assassination; Kent State shootings.	• Resist authority and are turned off by authority figures.
Orderly but overcrowded classrooms Strong authority figure; beginnings of interactivity.	• Prefer stable, orderly, risk-free learning environment, but want to interact with others. • See training as a benefit or perk.

• Organize training materials so that boomers can easily get the summary information and find more information if needed.

If you are a baby boomer working in the training field, check out the *Are You a Boomer Trainer?* sidebar for tips on updating your training.

Generation X

Known as the skeptical generation, Generation X (Gen X) includes workers born between 1966 and 1980.

Influential Events

This generation's formative years were marked by tragedy and disappointment (the Challenger disaster, the Clinton/Lewinsky scandal), the new American awareness of terrorism (the Lockerbie, Scotland, bombing of Pan Am flight 103), and cultural decline in the United States evidenced by media reports on AIDS, child abductions, and drug wars. At the same time, Generation X was at the forefront of the technical revolution, experiencing firsthand the birth of the Internet, cell phones, digital communications, computer-based training, and video games.

Impact on Learning

In general, Generation X members don't read as much as any of the other generations and are more likely to turn to the computer than to a book for their learning. This is the first generation to really embrace technology, so incorporate it into Gen X training whenever possible.

In training situations, they prefer to learn by doing. Gen Xers are happy to participate in role-play scenarios and enjoy receiving immediate feedback on their performance.

They prefer interactive learning and materials with lots of visuals, including sidebars, headlines, cartoons, illustrations, and inserts. This generation grew up with television and extensive stimulation; this has helped build their multitasking abilities.

For more, see the sidebar *Generation X Characteristics*.

Generation X Training Tips

- Build in self-directed learning opportunities. Assign individual research or projects. Provide online training and testing.

ARE YOU A BOOMER TRAINER?

If you are a baby boomer trainer, it may be time to reevaluate some of the old tried-and-true techniques that you have been using for years. As Marshall Goldsmith says, "What got you here won't get you there." If the people in your training classes are Gen X or Y, it is time to drop the traditional welcome-objectives-introduce-yourselves approach in favor of something a little more up to date.

Are you creating a classroom environment that mimics the one you experienced as an elementary school student? One in which Gen X or Y students are expected to sit still, listen, and focus for lengthy stretches of time, as presenter after presenter drones through an onslaught of PowerPoint slides? If so, it is time to

- set clear expectations for behavior and measurement criteria up front
- talk less, and let the learners talk more
- speed it up, then speed it up again
- let the learners figure it out, then teach each other
- be who you are and respect who they are; don't try to be one of them
- get rid of your old stories and get some new ones that Gen X and Y can relate to
- skip whatever is not critical, then put it where learners can access it if they need it
- explain your credentials; don't expect automatic respect based on your age or the fact that you are the trainer.

- Get to the point, efficiently. Banish anything in the curriculum that is being done just because it has always been done. Don't waste time.
- Avoid cliché and hyperbole, and make it relevant to their generation.
- Use technology wherever it makes sense.
- Build in lots of activity. Take field trips; schedule time for debates and games.
- Allow Gen Xers to figure things out on their own—give them the freedom, autonomy, and independence to come up with answers and alternatives.
- Communicate the benefits of the training and clearly establish the expectations from the beginning. Make sure what you are doing is relevant to their career goals.
- Build in options for getting the work done. Give them as much choice and autonomy as possible.
- Lighten up! Gen X loves humor, especially irreverent humor.
- Make it visually attractive. Avoid large blocks of text. Incorporate illustrations, cartoons, attractive graphic design, bullet points, and headers.

GENERATION X CHARACTERISTICS

Generation X	
Formative Events	**Learning Preferences**
Technical revolution Learned to read from Sesame Street; grew up with computers; began to utilize technology in classrooms.	• Want to use technology when possible. • Adaptive to change, comfortable with and seek out new approaches. • Want a variety of approaches to learning.
Single parent homes The first latchkey kids; learned early how to be independent and take care of themselves.	• Prefer independent, self-directed learning.
Tragedy and disappointment Watergate, Challenger disaster, AIDS, Persian Gulf, bankrupt Social Security.	• Enjoy less-authoritative teachers.
Societal stress AIDS, political scandal, urban and environmental degradation.	• Enjoy irreverent humor that pokes fun at societal ills.
Widespread layoffs of workaholic parents Distrust of the corporation; desire for work-life balance.	• Want control over schedule. • Resist workaholic approach to training. • See training and development as career security and a plus for the job market.

Generation Y

Generation Y (Gen Y) is the newest generation in the workplace and has seen an unprecedented technical revolution. This generation includes anyone born between 1981 and 2000.

Influential Events

Generation Y has grown up with terrorism and fear that is reinforced by the media in gory detail 24 hours a day, seven days a week. Baby boomer parents of Gen Ys were often frightened and protective. As a result, Gen Ys were placed in every possible team sport, lesson, organized activity, or supervised afterschool care setting, resulting in round-the-clock socialization and little unsupervised alone time. It is no wonder then that many Gen Ys prefer to work in groups and on teams. They like interaction with and affirmation from their supervisor, mentor, or teacher and crave lots and lots of recognition, praise, and feedback. Generation Ys like to be active participants in the learning process.

Generation Y Characteristics

Generation Y	
Formative Events	**Learning Preferences**
The information revolution	• Expect technology to be used in learning. • Want to be entertained and learn at the same time.
Violence and fear in the media Fear led parents to over-protect them; put into team sports, lessons, organized activities; always supervised.	• Prefer to learn in groups and teams. • Need lots of interaction with and feedback from facilitators, trainers, and managers.
Child focus and self-esteem The birth of "I like me" thinking; constant affirmation of self-worth.	• Require lots of reaffirmation that they are on the right track.
Stress and multitasking Highly scheduled lifestyle made Gen Yers very efficient; natural tendency is to complete many tasks as quickly as possible...sometimes at the expense of quality.	• Want clear expectations and instructions; efficient learning paths. • Impatient with "wasted" time, schedule changes, variance from the agenda. • Want to understand why they are expected to do something.
Diversity Racial, sexual, cultural diversity is a fact of life.	• Prefer group diversity.
Highly interactive classrooms	• Prefer collaborative classrooms. • Want peer-to-peer interaction. • Prefer fast-moving, interactive activities.

Impact on Learning

Generation Y members are accustomed to highly interactive learning. Their classrooms would appear chaotic to any veteran or baby boomer because they are designed for interaction, teamwork, and conversation. Classroom learning has evolved from sitting in rows with hands folded to a collaborative environment with students in small groups around tables. Their classes moved at a rapid pace, incorporating a variety of activities. These learners prefer collaborative classrooms and learning environments where they can interact with peers. While more than comfortable with technology, this generation grew up as readers and definitely reads more than Gen X.

One of the greatest outcomes of Gen Y's extensively scheduled existence is its ability to be highly effective at getting many things done in a concise period of time. This group is adept at finding the shortest route to the goal, and will look for easier, faster, and more direct ways to do things. They sometimes forfeit quality and depth for speed and efficiency and can be impatient with activities they believe are wasting time. This includes variations from a planned classroom agenda.

Generation Y members are among the most motivated learners if they see a direct benefit in what they are being taught, and among the least interested if the benefit is unclear. Generation Y places a high value on income; in fact, money is more important to this group than to any previous generation. Its members see education as a direct link to advancing their careers and making more money.

They also are accustomed to getting their information on demand, when they need it, from highly interactive and entertaining sources; they will not sit still for lengthy lectures and endless PowerPoint slides.

For more, see the sidebar *Generation Y Characteristics.*

Generation Y Training Tips

- Give Gen Y participants clear expectations up front, including behavioral expectations for the classroom.
- Be organized and provide a clear structure for the learning at the outset, including outlines, a syllabus, learning objectives, study guides, expectations, and how they will be evaluated.
- Tell them why the training matters, and make it relevant to their personal life and career goals.
- Stick to the agenda.
- Allow them to skip steps and find shortcuts; reward them for efficiency.
- Take time to link classroom learning to the big picture.
- Move quickly; then move faster.
- Provide lots of feedback, supervision, direction, and attention.
- Use technology and multimedia. Gen Y is very, very comfortable with technology and cannot imagine life without it. Try to have the latest in technology, and make sure you know how to use it.

- Make it fun and entertaining. Gen Y responds well to games, recognition, prizes, and visuals. Include multimedia, music, art, games, and creativity.
- Utilize experiential learning techniques that incorporate team interaction and hands-on participation, such as case studies, team projects, presentations, teaching others, and so on.
- Let them exchange information verbally or via texting to satisfy their need for social interaction.

IN THE CLASSROOM AND BEYOND

Many of the techniques that can enhance learning for one generation or another are simply the result of the application of good learning theory and design. When implemented, these techniques can enhance learning for everyone, regardless of age.

Use the following tips to bring together your new knowledge of the different generations.

■ *Develop Mentoring Programs*
Older workers are motivated by teaching others what they have learned through years of experience. Younger workers can benefit from opportunities to learn from those who have been in the workplace longer. These relationships can contribute to younger generations' ability to negotiate the political tides and prepare for promotions. Younger workers also can act as mentors to teach older employees about technical applications and to help develop faster, quicker, and more efficient ways of doing things.

■ *Encourage Ongoing Education*
For young and old alike, education opportunities can be motivating and excellent retention tools. Offer in-house education, tuition reimbursement, and professional development.

■ *Institute a Knowledge Retention Program*
Assign a task force to assess and develop strategies for passing along the knowledge currently held by your most vital senior employees.

■ *Avoid Being a Workaholic*
The natural tendency of many baby boomers is to show their commitment by working long hours. Younger generations may be less productive when forced to deliver "face time" or to spend long days and nights in a training room. Develop a reasonable agenda with a set end time, and stick to it. Take lots

of breaks to keep everyone awake. Adjust the workload back at the office so that participants don't see training as a barrier keeping them from getting their work done.

■ *Have the Generations Share Experiences*

Create multigenerational training groups. Assign seating and partners to ensure generational diversity in the groups. Assign tasks that older and younger generations can work on together, which will enhance the learning of both generations.

■ *Pay Attention to the Basics*

Schedule topics demanding the most attention and focus for the morning when attention is sharpest. Give 5- to 10-minute breaks every 90 minutes. Insist on nutritious food. Offer vegetables and fruit at breaks instead of cookies and ice cream. Provide lots of water and protein, like nuts, hard boiled eggs, dried peas, edamame, or cheese.

■ *Help Learners Internalize the Information*

Follow every major topic introduction with at least one transfer exercise that allows the learner to internalize the learning and put it into use. This satisfies Generation X's and Y's need for interactivity and participation, and gives older workers the chance to solidify and apply the learning.

■ *Use Diversity in Your Training Materials*

Make sure your visuals, role plays, case studies, examples, and exercises contain people from all generations represented in your workforce.

■ *Show Successful Role Models of Every Age*

Use employee presenters and external subject matter experts from a variety of age groups. Assign mentors from all generations.

■ *Create a Safe Environment*

An atmosphere of fear is not conducive to learning. Avoid activities that provoke insecurity. Encourage participation and discussion.

■ *Personalize the Training*

In general, younger workers prefer a fun and fast-paced learning environment while older workers require a comfortable, risk-free setting where their experience is valued. Mix participants up in small groups so they can learn from one another. Provide time for lots of questions, and look for feedback on whether the training is meeting their needs. Use situations and examples that workers might really encounter.

■ Use Role Play Wisely

Many older workers don't care for role play, while younger ones often like it so much they ask for more. Regardless of the participants' ages, use role play only in a safe environment. Don't put learners on the spot in potentially embarrassing situations in front of their peers, or worse, their managers. If you videotape, respect the learners' wishes about whether their manager should be allowed to view the tape.

■ Provide Clear Expectations

Don't expect other generations to share your values or behave by your standards, unless you clearly state those expectations. If you expect full attention and participation throughout class, say so, up front, at the beginning of class. If you expect that participants will not use their cell phones to text message during class, say so. If it drives you crazy that people show up late, visit websites, or answer emails on their PDA while you are conducting class, say so. If you have a certain dress code in mind, say so.

■ Use Technology

Interactive learning is a necessity, not an option, for younger workers, and most older workers are competent using technological applications as well. The range of creative training options is endless, and all generations can benefit from creative solutions to learning. Pair up younger and older workers to help each other use the technology, or use tech whizzes as mentors to teach technical applications to less savvy colleagues.

R-E-S-P-E-C-T

When it comes to generational diversity, respect is the key. Be who you are, respect who they are, and insist they respect each other. Remember, we can't fix each other, but we can adapt to the unique differences each generation brings to the workplace. When training, take time to set the ground rules for how you expect the generations to work together, and for the behaviors you expect to have exhibited in the classroom.

Be sensitive to the fact that all people, regardless of age, want to feel that they are important to the organization. Include them in the planning process and in the development of training materials. Finally, listen to their feedback, so you can adjust and improve learning and development for all the generations in your workforce.

BEST PRACTICES FOR ONBOARDING GEN Y

A strong onboarding process is a crucial part of getting employees to stay with your organization. Having an effective program for your younger workers is even more important, as Gen Y workers are quicker to move on if they feel the organization is not a good fit. Ensure your onboarding practices are Generation-Y appropriate with this job aid.

- We don't waste valuable classroom time on didactic presentations of background information. Instead, we insist on other options for delivering need-to-know content and save the classroom time for activities that help internalize the learning.
- We use on-demand formats such as databases, print manuals, online training, and so on for background information, such as operations overviews and fleet instructions.
- Our new employee orientation's goals are to get the employee comfortable with the organization, introduce the employee to the way the company operates, and help establish key relationships with company leaders and mentors.
- Our new employee orientation includes important need-to-know history, rules, people, language, culture, and performance expectations.
- We separate orientations from training when possible to help new employees get comfortable before they feel the pressure of going through training.
- We have done research with Gen Ys who have recently completed our onboarding process to gather feedback about whether our program is meeting their needs.
- We have an advisory board of Gen Ys that regularly reviews our onboarding program for effective Gen Y training principles.
- We allow plenty of time for the onboarding process to facilitate a smooth transition into our organization.
- We don't waste valuable classroom time on content that could be taught in other ways.
- We use on-demand formats for information that is nice-to-know versus need-to-know.
- We start with the end in mind: What do the learners absolutely need to know and when?
- We provide alternate routes to the same goal by allowing new employees to choose from an array of learning materials or experiences that will give them the background needed to become effective employees.
- We assign a mentor to every new employee and provide lots of opportunities for mentoring.
- We create multigenerational training groups that mix older generations with younger to enhance the learning of both generations.

RATE YOUR MULTIGENERATIONAL TRAINING

How does your classroom rate in terms of multigenerational training? Use the below assessment to find out if your training is on track for success or in need of some fine-tuning.

DIRECTIONS

Circle A—Always, S—Sometimes, or N—Never on the following scale:

Best Practices	Rating			Score
	Always	Sometimes	Never	
We provide equivalent opportunities for training and development for all of our employees, regardless of their age.	A	S	N	
We avoid very long days of training by developing a reasonable agenda and sticking to it.	A	S	N	
We schedule topics that demand the most attention for the morning training sessions.	A	S	N	
We give a 5- to 10-minute break at least every 90 minutes.	A	S	N	
We follow every major topic introduction with at least one interactive transfer exercise.	A	S	N	
We have a knowledge retention program currently in use.	A	S	N	
We offer mentoring opportunities to young and old alike.	A	S	N	
In our training sessions, we assign seats, partners, and breakout assignments rather than let participants choose their own.	A	S	N	
We offer nutritious food at breaks including vegetables, fruits, and plenty of water and protein.	A	S	N	
Our training materials, including visuals, role plays, and case studies, contain people from all generations in our workforce.	A	S	N	
Our training classes are a safe environment where participants can feel free to disagree without repercussion.	A	S	N	
Our expectations for training behavior and performance are set out at the beginning of the training session, both verbally and in writing.	A	S	N	
We use technology for many of our training applications.	A	S	N	
Our training showcases successful role models from all age groups.	A	S	N	
When we use role play, we are careful not to embarrass anyone or put anyone on the spot.	A	S	N	

SCORING

For each question, give yourself 5 points for A, 3 points for S, and 0 points for N.
If your score is:

60–75—Congratulations! You're doing an excellent job of meeting the learning needs of all the generations.

45–60—Your multigenerational training is OK, but could be improved by adding some of the best practices above.

Under 45—Your learners are asleep! Wake them up with the best practices above.

RACE AND DIVERSITY IN THE WORKFORCE

— *MARILYN Y. BYRD*

CHAPTER OVERVIEW

Race is represented under Title VII as a protected category of diversity in the workforce. However, limited discussion takes places on racism as a lingering social justice issue that persists as an outcome of race diversity in the contemporary workplace. This chapter will offer a historical perspective of race and will introduce sociological theoretical perspectives for studying racism as a consequence of race diversity in the workforce.

LEARNING OBJECTIVES

After reading this chapter, along with completing the chapter summary questions and the case discussion questions, you will be able to:

- Explain the distinctions between race and ethnicity
- Provide sociological theoretical perspectives of race
- Provide historical perspectives of racism in the United States
- Provide a social justice advocacy for studying racism

Race is a socially constructed category that denotes differences among people. The term is politically sustained to categorize people according to a specific group (Banton, 2000). Skin color is the most salient representation of how a person is judged based on race.

According to Banton (2000), new ways of explaining human difference have emerged but historical perspectives continue to influence racial thinking. This position is based on the variety of new ways that the word "race" is used, although the historical ones exist simultaneously. Historically, the word has been used to identify humans in terms of descent, biological type, and subspecies.

A racialized way of thinking has become popularized by a socialized application and through administration and political uses that "support old style racial explanations" (Banton, 2000, p. 53). The "conception of race as subspecies is not easily grasped by man . . . whereas race as type is much simpler and can be easily twisted to deal with conflicting evidence" (p. 58). Older concepts of race were grounded in notions based upon an individual's descent and then later to Dar-win's controversial theory of evolution. The contemporary concepts of race generally have been that of "race as type," although this conception was rendered invalid by Darwin's theory of evolution. Since the conception of race as descent was not earlier conceptions are still considered legitimate.

Ethnicity is a term that has emerged and in many cases has been used as an interchangeable term for race. The term *ethnicity* is a more contemporary way to denote different cultures and origins. But the term does not hold the historical implications for other cultures and origins that are associated with individuals of African descent. Another contemporary term being used is **people of color**. *People of color* is a term that is used to designate groups that are non-White and as such maintains a racial divide among groups (Zack, 2005).

However, the Black/White binary has been central to the discussion of race for several reasons. First, a divided country based on a system of slavery gave way to a state of physical freedom, but a segregated country still existed. Second, the struggle continued and led to the Civil Rights Movement, a historic period in the United States advocating for social justice by protesting the segregated practices that prevented Blacks from equal access and equal opportunity. Finally, the early 1960s was a period of civil unrest in the United States and further highlighted the racial divide between Black and White racial groups and brought about a huge movement for civil rights.

Civil rights are enforceable rights or privileges that if interfered with by another gives rise to an action for injury (Cornell University Law School, 2010). During this period of time in society, the Black/White binary persisted from the lingering effects of slavery and continues to be the major cause of racism.

SOCIOLOGICAL THEORETICAL PERSPECTIVES FOR STUDYING RACE

A number of social science theorists have sought to offer theories that will lend a better understanding of race and ethnicity. Constructionist and structural theories both acknowledge that race and ethnicity are social constructs that shape how people are situated within the larger society. Further, both approaches are concerned with resolving the dilemma of what race and ethnicity mean and how society in general perceives these socially constructed notions. Both approaches recognize group

TABLE 4.1 Contrasts of Constructionist and Structural Approaches to Race and Ethnicity

CONSTRUCTIONIST	STRUCTURAL
Focus on group characteristics	Focus on antagonisms created by group difference
Narrow view of racism	Broad view of racism
Focus on culture, ideology, and identity	Focus on power
By-product of economic, political, and social forces	Product of economic, political, and social forces
Groups contribute in the making and creating of their identities	Groups categorized
Static	Changing
Free-floating ideology	Structural and embedded
Psychological and irrational	Systemic and rational
Historicity	Contemporary structure
Overt behavior	Overt and covert behavior

identity and the categorization of a group or population of people. Table 4.1 identifies some major differences between structural and constructionist approaches to race and ethnicity (Bonilla-Silva, 1997; Loveman, 1997).

The constructionist perspective has been the prevailing notion for studying race and ethnicity in the social sciences. However, we need a deeper understanding of race that explains the system of racism. The structural approaches to race and ethnicity seek to study how power and privilege continue to sustain a racial structure.

According to the constructionist approach, race and ethnicity are categories, and specific identities of human beings "trying to solve problems, defend or enhance their positions, justify their actions, establish meanings, achieve understanding, or otherwise negotiate their way through the world in which they live" (Cornell & Hartmann, 1998, p. xviii). Constructionists emphasize ideological and cultural processes for understanding race and ethnicity. Structuralists will say that constructionist approaches have a narrow view of racism. As a result, the constructionist approach does not adequately address the problem of racism, which is deeply embedded within institutionalized practices within society. Structural approaches challenge systems that allow antagonisms stemming from racism to exist—systems that block mobility for marginalized people who encounter a hierarchy in which Whites have political and economic power (Waters, 1999). Structural approaches to understanding race and ethnicity suggest that power structures are responsible for the gaps in economic disparity, unemployment, poverty, and access to resources that sustain life. Thinking of race in terms of structure means that we are acknowledging the privilege of some and thus giving credence to racial hierarchy.

The constructionists believe that racial and ethnic groups are socially constructed and are by-products of economic, political, or social forces. As those forces change, so do their racial and ethnic products (Cornell & Hartmann, 1998). Structuralists would add that the creation of racism is a by-product of economic, political, and social forces' actions upon race and ethnicity.

Constructionists believe in a free-floating ideology—that groups contribute to the making and sustaining of their identities. Therefore, constructionists are concerned with how groups form and construct identity, and how people within groups conceptualize themselves and others (Cornell & Hartmann, 1998). Theorists that speak from the constructionist paradigm believe that as certain groups contend with situations that arise within their social arenas, identities are constructed as people try to make sense of their world. Racial categories then "become socially significant to the extent they are used to organize and interpret experience, to form social relations, and to organize individual and collective action" (p. 24). Structuralists would add that as time passes, categories are subject to change, particularly as people struggle to assign other people to them. As products of social change, circumstance, human interpretation, and social action, race and ethnicity are not static, but rather variable, diverse, and contingent upon social arenas such as politics, labor markets, residential space, social institutions, culture, and daily experience (Cornell & Hartmann, 1998). Furthermore, racial categories are used as a foundation for government action and other practices where justification to distinguish people is presumed necessary.

Some constructionists' approaches to race and ethnicity are grounded in historical conceptions that slavery is responsible for an irrational, rigid, and overt form of racism (Bonilla-Silva, 1997). Structuralist approaches will say that racism today is more covert and subtle in nature due to its embedded position within institutionalized practices that are controlled by Whites. Theorists that are advancing the structural approach to race maintain racial discrimination is no longer one of inequality but rather one of racial mistreatment within the structures of society. The inequality that is taking place now occurs behind closed doors. Those who hold the power are making decisions that affect people of color. In the United States, that power typically belongs to Whites.

SELECTED THEORIES FROM THE CONSTRUCTIONIST AND STRUCTURAL APPROACHES

The constructionist and structural approaches to race and ethnicity represent the worldviews that generally agree upon basic assumptions. However some theorists, while speaking from these paradigms, advance their own interpretations in an effort to render a deeper understanding of how race and ethnicity

TABLE 4.2   Selected Constructionist and Structural Theories

CONSTRUCTIONIST	STRUCTURAL
Omi & Winant (racial formation)	Feagin (systemic racism: theory of oppression)
Murji & Solomos (racialization)	Lewis (Whiteness)
Nagel (ethnic identity)	Bonilla-Silva (racialized social systems)

shape our lives. Table 4.2 represents six selected theories or interpretations to identify how the different worldviews or paradigms represent the study of race.

RACIAL FORMATION

The racial formation theory suggested by Omi and Winant (1994) suggests that to some extent we all learn some technique to categorize people whether we are consciously aware of it or not. This satisfies a need to comprehend, explain, and determine social actions. But to understand how to combat racial discrimination that might occur through social action and how to dismantle the systems that tolerate and perpetuate racial discrimination, we should consider the socio-historical contexts of race. The racial formation theory seeks to address the topics of historicity, group identity, and social comprehensiveness as well as account for the way individuals and groups have to manage conflictual racial meanings in everyday experiences (Winant, 2000) that is lacking in structural approaches. Racial formation is produced as the meaning of race changes through the practice of societal groups. Racial formation theory suggest that in the United States race and ethnicity should be understood as constructs of social organization that are politically determined by the state.

RACIALIZATION

Bonilla-Silva (1997) presents a strong argument from a structural perspective for a theorization of race and ethnicity that uses the concept of racialization. Revisiting the notion of racialization, an idea advanced by Banton (1979), Murji and Solomos (2005) find this idea is useful in "describing the processes by which racial meanings are attached to particular issues and the manner in which race appears to be a key factor in the ways they are defined and understood" (p. 3). However, Murji and Solomos do not offer a theoretical perspective. Rather, they incite dialogue concerning the multiple uses of racialization—as "a problematic, a framework, or as a process" (p. 4). This brings to light the question: If we cannot be clear about what the process of racialization is, we cannot be clear as to whether racialization captures the purpose and essence for which it is intended at a given point in time.

ETHNIC IDENTITY

Nagel's (1994) study of ethnic identity is a constructionist approach that addresses how ethnic groups are "negotiated, defined and produced through social interaction inside and outside ethnic communities" (p. 152). Nagel does not emphasize race and ethnicity, but rather ethnicity and culture. In doing so, the element of historicity is taken away but the dimension of boundaries is added. Nagel's approach is useful for accommodating the issue of immigration. "Boundaries determine who is a member and who is not and designates which ethnic categories are available for individual identification at any point in time" (p. 154). But if this is the case, then Nagel's approach has structural implications as well, because designating categories then becomes a process that is regulated by the state.

THEORY OF OPPRESSION

Feagin (2006) advances a structural approach based on a theory of oppression. Feagin points out that while discrimination has been made illegal, institutionalized practices such as employment, education, and other practices within the public domain still allow racism. These structures dominate society because "white officials at all levels of the government who rarely take aggressive action to significantly reduce racial discrimination in the U.S." (p. 24) typically control them.

Feagin's (2006) approach challenges constructionists to broaden their perspective of historicity and see the reality that oppression experienced during slavery lingers on in a more contemporary form of oppression embedded within structural systems. This oppression is being fed by the large scale wealth-generating resources of White Americans and through the resources that grant privilege to some while continuing to marginalize others. Feagin's approach departs from the constructionist view in that he seeks to give voice to the "experiences, views, understandings, and interests of those oppressed as well as the experiences, views, and understanding, and interests of their oppressors" (p. 9). Structural systems such as economic, political, educational, media, and public institutions in the United States continue to oppress because these systems decide who have the power and how groups are situated within these systems and institutions.

STUDY OF WHITENESS

Lewis (2004) suggests that all people within society are racialized, including Whites. Lewis (2004) acknowledges the structure of racial hierarchy, but questions, "How can race be structural and embedded, yet superficial, arbitrary and whimsical, shifting with times and circumstances. Here, Lewis is challenging both the structural and constructionist approaches. Studies of race and ethnicity do not adequately account for Whiteness, or how Whites are a part of the structure that have created and sustained a racialized society. "Understanding the relationship between the daily performance of race and larger racial structure is key to our understanding of how race works more generally and to how it shapes the lives of whites" (p. 629). The literature on race and ethnicity tends to focus on understanding these constructs from the perspectives of the marginalized groups, leaving us with limited insight on the construct of "Whiteness."

STRUCTURAL THEORY

Bonilla-Silva (1997) argues, "the central problem of the various approaches to the study of racial phenomena is their lack of a structural theory of racism" (p. 465). Bonilla-Silva contends that in order to explain the social construction of race, we must understand the structural notion of race. Bonilla-Silva's position is that when race emerged as a social construct, this racialized system resulted in privileging some groups over others. In the case of U.S. society, Whites assume a privilege over Blacks and other people of color. From Bonilla-Silva's perspective, Whites are the major actors in sustaining a racial social system because, in doing so, they reap the benefits of a racial order, whereas members defined as belonging to subordinate groups struggle to challenge and change the racial status quo.

Bonilla-Silva (2003) challenges a **color-blind** ideology that difference is seen, but not acknowledged as being different. According to Bonilla-Silva, a color-blind ideology:

- Operates on the idea of sameness, with Whiteness being the norm
- Defines experiences and sets standards according to the norm
- Results in an avoidance of the topic of racism

As a result, a color-blind ideology curtails the topic of racism and accusations of racial discrimination, acting as a curtain for racists to hide their racial views. Furthermore, this ideology serves as a tool in challenging and attacking legal rights that have been gained by minority groups. Bonilla-Silva (2003) suggests rather than attempting to sell the idea of nonracism, we should adopt the notion of antiracism.

The structural theory developed by Bonilla-Silva (1997) comes close to presenting a coherent framework for studying race and ethnicity. The theory is based on "concepts elaborated by the institutionalist, the internal colonial, and the racial formation perspectives" (p. 467), contending that race be studied from the viewpoint of racism. While Bonilla-Silva's theory does not aim to give a universal explanation of race and ethnicity, the intention is to provoke dialogue that should direct theorization toward that goal.

RACISM IN THE UNITED STATES

Racism is a process whereby socialized racist notions become integrated with actions and practices in such a way that these actions and practices become actualized and reinforced through routine situations (Essed, 1991). In the workplace, these situations can occur through individual actions or institutional practices. Although there has been progress, racism continues to persist, and for the most part, people of color are perceived as unequal by White America.

Racism is racial prejudice sustained by power, privilege, and resources (Feagin & Sikes, 1994). This prejudice perpetuates racism and is rationalized by the belief that a group's abilities, values, and culture are attributed to physical features such as skin color. Modern-day racism encompasses subtle as well as covert acts of White bigots and is "inescapable in the everyday worlds of African Americans. Almost any encounter with Whites, in workplaces, schools, neighborhoods, and public places can mean a confrontation with racism" (p. 4). Essed (1991) theorized racism as a process that has become routine in ordinary, everyday actions and practices. The term *racism* is also related to concepts such as discrimination, prejudice, and stereotypes (Dovidio, Brigham, Johnson, & Gaertner, 1996), but it is more encompassing than any of these. Dovidio et al. further stated that the actions of discrimination, prejudice, and stereotypes can also be viewed as unjust social behaviors, attitudes, or beliefs. In its very essence, racism involves not only negative attitudes and beliefs but also the social power to disadvantage some groups of people and at the same time it offers advantages to other groups.

Jones (1997) offered the perspective that there are two types of racism at the social levels. The first type is individual racism, which relates to the interplay of stereotypes, prejudices, and discrimination that manifest and support unequal treatment and practices between members of diverse groups. The second is institutional racism, which refers to the undeliberate handling or acceptance of institutional procedures (e.g., qualifying for a home mortgage, unfair hiring practices, inequitable admissions criteria) that have unjustly limited the opportunities of certain groups of people.

INDIVIDUAL RACISM

According to Brigham (1993), individual racism can be expressed both overtly and covertly. Overt racism is intentional and the perpetrator's racist motives are clearly expressed (Ridley, 2005). On the other hand, covert racism is more subtle or hidden and the perpetrator's motives are difficult to detect. Many contemporary approaches to individual racism acknowledge the persistence of overt, intentional forms of racism but also consider the automatic or unconscious processes and indirect expressions of bias as represented by covert racism.

In contrast to overt and covert racism, Dovidio and Gaertner (1998) identified aversive racism, which represents a subtle, often unintentional, form of bias. This bias projects itself through harsh racial feelings and beliefs that are developed unconsciously. Dovidio and Gaertner further asserted that, because of these unconscious biases, aversive racism suggests that individuals may often participate in acts of discrimination while maintaining a positive opinion of one's self.

McConahay (1986) conceptualized a theory of modern racism that provides a tool to measure the dimensions of cognitive racial attitudes. The theory is based on the notion that negative attitudes formed by Whites regarding African Americans are affective and are acquired early in life. Modern racism posits four assumptions. First, people with racist attitudes maintain the position that racism no longer exists. Second, people with racist attitudes believe that minorities use tactics such as affirmative action to gain access to opportunities that would be otherwise unattainable. Third, people with racist attitudes maintain that Blacks are too aggressive in using laws such as affirmative action to their advantage. Finally, people with racist attitudes believe that Blacks who utilize policies such as affirmative action are undeserving. Racism in overt and covert forms can contribute to social policies that form the basis of institutional racism.

INSTITUTIONAL RACISM

According to Klinker and Smith (1999), institutional racism reflects the differential effects of policies, practices, and laws on members of certain racial groups. Historically, institutional racism developed from intentional racism, such as limiting immigration and the voting rights of certain racial groups. Another historical example highlights how the majority group created and justified laws that enabled them to enslave Africans and African Americans and confiscate property from indigenous tribes (Klinker & Smith, 1999). While Fields (1990) suggested that institutional racism is: (1) independent of individual racism and (2) requires the active support of individuals that have an awareness or intention to discriminate, Feagin and Vera (1995) stated that the concept of institutional racism is not recognized as racially unfair because it is ingrained into policies and laws, which suggests that it is morally right. However, what is seen as fair and just can and does vary according to one's perspective.

PERSISTENCE OF RACISM IN THE WORKPLACE

According to Bonilla-Silva (2003), avoiding discussions of racism allows individuals to hide their true racial viewpoints, which is another way that the majority viewpoint remains. Avoiding or ignoring the topic of racism suggests that the topic is either too volatile or that it is not serious enough to engage in conversations.

A popular misconception is that post– **civil rights** laws and legislation have eradicated racism. Post–civil rights laws and legislation mandating equal opportunity have created a color-blind ideology that operates on the notion of sameness (Bonilla-Silva, 2003). However this notion is a mechanism for avoiding discussions of racism and conceals the individual and institutional levels in which racism is still prevalent. Acknowledging racism is necessary not only for those subjected to the experience (individual level) but also for those involved in policymaking practices and procedures (institutional level).

Another misconception is that the election of the first African American president in 2008 is an indicator that racism no longer exists (Reed & Louis, 2009). However, incidents of alleged racism in the workplace persist. In July 2009, the *Houston Chronicle* reported two female firefighters recently returned to their living quarters to find racial and sexual graffiti in their personal spaces. KTVT in Dallas/Fort Worth reported March 12, 2009, that Confederate flags, racist graffiti, and a hangman's noose were discovered in various parts of Turner Industries, a pipe factory in Paris, Texas. On July 29, 2009, the *State Journal-Register* in Springfield, Illinois, reported a noose that was discovered hanging in a workspace at the City Water, Light, and Power. To African American people, these symbols are connected to a period of time in this country when African American people were subjected to inhumane and egregious acts of hate. Therefore, the recurrence of these symbols in contemporary times conveys a subtle meaning of racism.

DiversityInc, reported that during the 2012 election, the growing popularity of social media helped to spread racial hatred before and after the re-election of President Obama. Because of the multiple modes of social media available, it is likely that stereotypical images pervade the workplace and threaten the goal of an inclusive workplace to make all people feel welcomed and respected. According to DiversityInc, derogatory depictions of the President as a monkey or with exaggerated physical features along with other demeaning attacks on the President and Michelle Obama targeted their identity as African Americans rather than targeting their political views or affiliation. Attacking the President of the United States in such a blatant, stereotypical, racist, and disrespectful way casts a shadow on the prevalence of racism in society.

UNCOVERING RACISM IN DIVERSITY

Generally, companies, businesses, and organizations recognize and acknowledge their commitments and efforts in promoting diversity in the workplace. In fact, diversity initiatives are recognized as one indicator of success for companies appearing on *Fortune's* Best Companies to Work For list. Rarely discussed or acknowledged, however, are the issues that emerge from a diverse workforce. The nature of diversity among groups and the perceptions and assumptions about certain racial groups can produce negative attitudes and behaviors. To truly appreciate, value, and embrace diversity requires changes in negative attitudes and behaviors that result in the persistence of racism in institutional and organizational settings (Thomas, 1991, 2005). There-fore, moving organizations toward a state of valuing and appreciating diversity is counterproductive if acts of racism continue to persist.

Bernier and Rocco (2003) argued that rarely have the effects of race and racism been used to study diversity and the issues that emerge from diversity in the workplace. Consequently, diversity, in terms of race, within organizations cannot be leveraged unless there is an understanding of the historical and contemporary causes of racism. Although organizations are making strides to be viewed as diversity-focused, the state of being diverse often places individuals into categories that leave them open to being labeled, stigmatized, and vulnerable to actions and perceptions based on that category. Deitch et al. (2003) reported that modern acts of racism such as unwelcoming attitudes, unwillingness or refusal to cooperate, and avoidance or refusal to acknowledge have replaced the more blatant and outward displays of racism; however, this statement is being challenged in wake of the reappearance of blatant acts like nooses, racial graffiti, and displaying of the Confederate flag. These adverse actions and perceptions are discriminatory, prejudicial, and stereotypical and can all permeate from racism.

EMERGING PERSPECTIVES ON RACISM AS A SOCIAL JUSTICE ISSUE

Racism is a social justice issue that served as a historical root of workforce diversity and training in the United States (Cox, 1993). However, Jane Elliott, a noted diversity trainer, says (PBS, 2010):

> . . . we are still conditioning people in this country and, indeed, all over the globe to the myth of white superiority. We are constantly being told that we don't have racism in this country anymore, but most of the people who are saying that are white.

Furthermore, as long as we continue to use certain language (such as race and ethnicity) certain groups in society will continue to be viewed in terms of a specific category. Racialized language feeds the system of racism and allows it to persist through political categorization and institutionalized practices within our society.

Realistically speaking, changing large systems that control the public domain from racialized thinking would be a slow and arduous act. Assigning people to a "race" has been engrained in this society for years. We are categorized (racialized) immediately from birth, and the birth document becomes an immediate identifier as to who we are. To contest this categorization would still remain a government-controlled process, which means how a person experiences race remains under the power and control of the state. Shifting this power from the state is a matter for social advocacy and perhaps a new social movement.

CHAPTER SUMMARY

The word *race* has had various historical meanings. However, the word has emerged in more contemporary terms to categorize individuals according to groups. In doing so, certain groups maintain a marginalized status in society based on group affiliation. Although legislation was passed to protect individuals based on race as well as other diverse categories, attitudes and behaviors formed from nonacceptance of individuals continue. In the workplace, these attitudes play out in form of verbal or physical actions that communicate the practice of racism. Leadership within organizations is responsible for ensuring socially just organizations whereby all individuals feel safe and welcomed.

DEFINITION OF KEY TERMS

Civil rights—A civil right is an enforceable right or privilege that if interfered with by another gives rise to an action for injury.

Civil Rights Movement—A social justice movement in the United States in the early 1960s advocating equal access and equal opportunity for Black Americans.

Color-blind—Difference is seen but not acknowledged as being different; attempting to promote a nonracist policy.

Constructionist theory—Explains racial and ethnic groups as socially constructed based on by-products of economic, political, or social forces. As those forces change, so do the racial and ethnic by-products.

Ethnicity—Ethnicity is a more contemporary way to denote different cultures and origins, including people of color.

Individual racism—Interplay of stereotypes, prejudices, and discrimination that manifest and support unequal treatment and practices between members of diverse groups.

Institutional racism—Differential effects of policies, practices, and laws on members of certain racial groups; deliberate or undeliberate handling or acceptance of institutional procedures (e.g., qualifying for a home mortgage, unfair hiring practices, inequitable admissions criteria) that have unjustly limited the opportunities of certain groups of people.

People of color—A term used to designate groups that are non-White.

Race—Socially constructed category that denotes differences among people and is politically sustained to assign people to categories.

Racialization—Processes by which racial meanings are attached to particular issues and the manner in which race appears to be a key factor in the ways they are defined and understood.

Racism—Process whereby socialized racist notions become integrated with actions and practices in such a way that these actions and practices become actualized and reinforced through routine situations.

Structural theory—Explains racism as a by-product of economic, political, and social forces' actions upon race and ethnicity.

CRITICAL-THINKING DISCUSSION QUESTIONS

1. Discuss how the historical development of racial groups contributes to sustaining racism in the United States.
2. Compare and contrast the constructionist and structural theories of race.
3. Discuss ways that institutional racism could exist in the workforce. Give specific examples.
4. Discuss ways that individual racism could exist in the workforce. Give specific examples.

LEGAL PERSPECTIVES

In June 2013, allegations of systemic racism were filed against Paula Deen, a world-renowned chef, for using the "N" word. Employees also reported to the Rainbow/PUSH Coalition, a social change organization, that Blacks were paid disproportionately from Whites and received fewer opportunities for advancement.

In September 2012, the Equal Employment Opportunity Commission (EEOC) obtained a settlement of $630,000 filed against a California trucking firm and its successor on the behalf of African American, Latino, and East Indian workers. The workers alleged discrimination on the basis of race, national origin, and religion. In the original complaint, management and employees were alleged to have subjected drivers to racial slurs, such as using the "N" word when referring to Black drivers, calling East Indian drivers "Taliban" or "camel drivers," and using the word "spic" when referring to a Latino manager. White workers were also alleged to be given more favorable job assignments than non-Whites.

In May 2008, the Equal Employment Opportunity Commission (EEOC) obtained a settlement of $1.65 million in a racial harassment case filed against a general contractor and its subsidiaries on behalf of a class of African American employees who were subjected to egregious racial harassment at a construction site in Bethlehem, Pennsylvania. The harassment included a life-size noose made of heavy rope hung from a beam in a class member's work area for at least 10 days before it was removed; the regular use of the "N" word; and racially offensive comments made to Black individuals, including "I think everybody should own one," "Black people are no good and you can't trust them," and "Black people can't read or write." Additionally, racist graffiti was written in portable toilets, with terms such as "coon," "if u not white u not right," "white power," "KKK," and "I love the Ku Klux Klan." Additional remedies were injunctive relief enjoining each defendant from engaging in racial harassment or retaliation, antidiscrimination training, the posting of a notice about the settlement, and reporting complaints of racial harassment to the EEOC for monitoring. (*Source*: www.eeoc.gov/eeoc/initiatives/e-race/caselist.cfm)

REFERENCES

Banton, M. (1979). Analytical and folk concepts of race and ethnicity. *Ethnic & Racial Studies, 2* (2), 127–138.

Banton, M. (2000). The idiom of race: A critique of presentation. In L. Back & J. Solomos (Eds.), *Theories of race and racism* (pp. 53–63). London: Routledge.

Bernier, J. D., & Rocco, T. S. (2003). Working in the margins of Critical Race Theory and HRD. *Proceedings of the 2003 Midwest Research to Practice Conference in Adult, Continuing, and Community Education* (pp. 13–18). Colum-bus: The Ohio State University.

Bonilla-Silva, E. (1997). Rethinking racism. *American Sociological Review, 62*, 465–79.

Bonilla-Silva, E. (2003). *Racism without racists: Color blind racism and the persistence of racial inequality in the United States.* New York: Rowman & Littlefield.

Brigham, J. C. (1993). College students' racial attitudes. *Journal of Applied Social Psychology, 23*, 1933–1967.

Cornell, S. E., & Hartmann, D. (1998). *Ethnicity and race: Making identities in a changing world.* Thousand Oaks, CA: Pine Forge Press.

Cornell University Law School (2010). Retrieved from http://topics.law.cornell.edu/wex/Civil_rights

Cox, T., Jr. (1993). *Cultural diversity in organizations: Theory, research and practice.* San Francisco: Berrett-Koehler.

Deitch, E. A., Barsky, A., Butz, R. M., Chan, S., Brief, A. P., & Bradley, J. C. (2003). Subtle yet significant: The existence and impact of everyday racial discrimination in the workplace. *Human Relations, 56* (11), 1299–1324.

DiversityInc (2012). Racist Obama Facebook pages & your office: What do you need to know? Retreived June 26, 2013, from: www.diversityinc.com/diversity-management/racist-obama-facebook-pages-your-office-what-do-you-need-to-know/

Dovidio, J. F., Brigham, J. C., Johnson, B. T., & Gaertner, S. L. (1996). Stereotyping, prejudice, and discrimination: Another look. In N. Macrae, M. Hewstone, & C. Stangor (Eds.), *Confronting racism: The problem and the response* (pp. 3–32). Newbury Park, CA: Sage.

Dovidio, J. F., & Gaertner, S. L. (1998). On the nature of contemporary prejudice: The causes, consequences, and challenges of aversive racism. In J. Eberhardt & S. T. Fiske (Eds.), *Confronting racism: The problem and the response* (pp. 3–32). Newbury Park, CA: Sage.

Essed, P. (1991). *Understanding everyday racism: An interdisciplinary theory.* Newbury Park, CA: Sage.

Feagin, J. (2006). *Systemic racism: A theory of oppression.* London: Routledge.

Feagin, J. R., & Sikes, M. P. (1994). *Living with racism: The Black middle-class experience.* Boston: Beacon Press.

Feagin, J. R., & Vera, H. (1995). *White racism.* New York: Routledge.

Fields, B. (1990). Slavery, race and ideology in the United States of America. *New Left Review, 181.*

Jones, J. M. (1997). *Prejudice and racism* (2nd ed.). New York: McGraw-Hill. Klinker, P. A., & Smith, R. M. (1999). *The unsteady march: The rise and decline of American commitments to racial equality.* New York: Free Press.

Lewis, A. (2004). What group?: Studying whites and whiteness in the era of color blindness. *Sociological Theory, (22)*4, 623–464.

Loveman, M. (1997). Is race essential? A comment on Bonilla-Silva. *American Sociological Review, 64* (6), 891–898.

McConahay, J. B. (1986). Modern racism and ambivalence, and the modern racism scale. In J. F. Dovidio & S. L. Gaertner (Eds.), *Prejudice, discrimination, and racism* (pp. 91–125). Orlando, FL: Academic Press.

Murji, K., & Solomos, J. (Eds.) (2005). *Racialization: Studies in theory and practice.* Oxford: Oxford University Press.

Nagel, J. (1994). Constructing ethnicity: Creating and recreating ethnic identity and culture. *Social Problems, 41* (1), 152–176.

Omi, M., & Winant, H. (1994). *Racial formation in the United States: From the 1960s to the 1990s.* London: Routledge.

PBS (2010). A class divided. Retrieved from www.pbs.org/wgbh/pages/frontline/shows/divided/etc/crusade.html

Reed, W. L., & Louis, B. M. (2009). No more excuses: Problematic responses to Barack Obama's election. *Journal of Africana Studies, 13* (2), 97–109. doi:10.1007/s12111–009–9088–3

Ridley, C. R. (2005). *Overcoming unintentional racism in counseling and therapy.* Thousand Oaks, CA: Sage.

Thomas, R. R. (1991). *Beyond race and gender.* New York: AMACOM.

Thomas, R. R. (2005). *Building on the promise of diversity: How can we move to the next level in our workplaces, our communities, and our society?* New York: AMACOM.

Waters, M. C. (1999). Explaining the comfort factor: West Indian Immigrants confront American race relations. In M. Lamont (Ed.), *Cultural territories of race: Black and White boundaries* (pp. 63–96). Chicago: University of Chicago Press.

Winant, H. (2000). The theoretical status of the concept of race. In L. Back & J. Solomos (Eds.), *Theories of race and racism* (pp. 181–190). London: Routledge.

Zack, N. (2005). *Thinking about race.* Florence, KY: Wadsworth Publishing, Cengage Learning.

READING CREDITS

1. R. Edward Freeman, Patricia H. Werhane, and Andrew C. Wicks, "Diversity," pp. 1-6. Copyright © 2002 by Darden Business Publishing. Reprinted with permission.

2. Cedric Herring, "Diversity = Dollars," *Americas Quarterly*, vol. 6, no. 3, pp. 69-72. Copyright © 2012 by Americas Society / Council of the Americas. Reprinted with permission. Provided by ProQuest LLC. All rights reserved.

3. Tammy A. Turner-Vorbeck, "Expanding Multicultural Education to Include Family Diversity," *Multicultural Education*, vol. 20, issue 34, pp. 24–28, 110. Copyright © 2013 by Caddo Gap Press. Reprinted with permission. Provided by ProQuest LLC. All rights reserved.

4. Kim A. Rowe, "Training Across Generations." Copyright © 2008 by Association for Talent Development (ATD). Reprinted with permission.

5. Marilyn Y. Byrd, "Race and Diversity in the Workforce," *Diversity in the Workforce: Current Issues and Emerging Trends*, ed. Marilyn Y. Byrd and Chaunda L. Scott, pp. 75–92. Copyright © 2014 by Taylor & Francis Group. Reprinted with permission.

REFERENCES

Alexander, M. (2010). *The new Jim Crow: Mass incarceration in the age of colorblindness*. New York: New Press.

Anastasia. (2010, March 22). 7 barriers to active listening: Why we don't listen as well as we could. *Lawsagna* [blog]. Retrieved from http://lawsagna.typepad.com/lawsagna/2010/03/7-barriers-to-active-listening-why-we-dont-listen-as-well-as-we-could.html

Anthes, E. (2012, November 5). The everyday fear zone. *Psychology Today*. Retrieved from https://www.psychologytoday.com/articles/201211/the-everyday-fear-zone

Argyle, M., Salter, V., Nicholson, H., Williams, M., & Burgess, P. (1970). The communication of interior and superior attitudes by verbal and non-verbal signals. *British Journal of Clinical Psychology, 9*(3) 222–231.

Avery-Stoss, J. (2015, October 5). Barriers to effective listening. *Livestrong*. Retrieved from http://www.livestrong.com/article/75715-barriers-effective-listening-skills

Blanchard, K. (2006, March, 14). *Interview,* Chapel Hill, North Carolina.

Bonilla-Silva, E. (2006) "*Racism Without Racist: Colorblind Racism and the Persistence of Racial Inequality in the United States.*" Rowman Littlefield Publishers; Lanhain, Maryland. Pp.3, 55–57.

Braun, S. (2014, January 31). Fact check: NSA leaks worst intelligence breach? *Washington Times*. Retrieved from http://www.washingtontimes.com/news/2014/jan/31/fact-check-nsa-leaks-worst-intelligence-breach

Cacioppo, J., Hager, J., & Ekman, P. (1992). NSF Report on Facial Expressions.

Carnegie, D. (1936). *How to win friends and influence people*. New York: Simon & Schuster.

Clayton, R. (2013, June 10). Facebook, divorce linked in new study. *Huffington Post*. Retrieved from http://www.huffingtonpost.com/2013/06/06/facebook-divorce-linked-i_n_3399727.html.

Collins, P.H. (2005). *Black Sexual Politics: African Americans, Gender and the New Racism*. Routledge Press. Pp. 96–99).

Coty, J. (2016). Employee social media posts put Charlotte companies on guard. Retrieved from **http://www.charlotteobserver.com/news/business/article85138967.html.** July 21, 2016.

Covey, S. R. (1989). *The 7 habits of highly successful people.* New York: Simon & Schuster.

Daniel-Tatum, B. (1997). *Why are all the Black kids sitting together in the cafeteria? And other conversations about race.* New York: Basic Books.

Das, P. (2009, December 23). Facebook is the new cause of divorce. *Tech Journal.* Retrieved from http://thetechjournal.com/internet/facebook-is-the-new-cause-of-divorce.xhtml

Definition of "Friend." In Merriam-Webster On-line Dictionary. Retrieved from http://www.merriam-webster.com.

Dennis, A. (2013, July 8). Paula Deen: What will she do next? *People.* Retrieved from http://www.people.com/people/archive/article/0,,20715448,00.html

Ekman, P. (2016). *"What scientists who study emotion agree about."* Perspectives on Psychological Science 11(1) 31–34.

Ekman, P., & Friesen. (1975). Are Facial Expressions Universal? http://greatergood.berkeley.edu/article/item/are_facial_expressions_universal

Facebook. (n.d.). Mission statement. Retrieved from https://www.facebook.com/facebook/info?tab=page_info

Family Care Foundation (FCF). (2011). If the world were a village of 100 people. Retrieved from http://www.familycare.org/special-interest/if-the-world-were-a-village-of-100-people

Friend. (n.d.). In *Merriam-Webster.* Retrieved from http://www.merriam-webster.com/dictionary/friend

Gates, H. L. (Narrator). (2013). *African American Lives* [documentary miniseries]. PBS. Available from

Greenwood, D. *"Understanding the Oscar Obsession: In Between the Popcorn and the Snark lies Something More."* Psychology Today. Feb, 24, 2014. Retrieved from https://www.psychologytoday.com/blog/mirror-mirror/201402/understanding-the-oscar-obsession.

Gregory, S. (2012, February 11). It's official: Linsanity is for real. *Time.* Retrieved from http://newsfeed.time.com/2012/02/11/its-official-linsanity-is-for-real

Hager J. C., & Ekman, P. (1995). *"Essential behavioral science of the face and gesture that computer scientist need to know."* Retrieved from http://citeseerx.ist.psu.edu/showciting?cid=1773144

Hamilton, W., & Lopez, R. (2014, January 10). Target says data breach is far larger than first estimated. *L.A. Times.* Retrieved from http://articles.latimes.com/2014/jan/10/business/la-fi-target-breach-20140111

Heathfield, S. M. (2016, June 28). Tips for understanding nonverbal communication: Listen with your eyes. About.com Human Resources. Retrieved from http://humanresources.about.com/od/interpersonalcommunicatio1/a/nonverbal_com.htm

Hsu, T. (2014, January 29). Target traces data breach to credentials stolen from vendor. *L.A. Times.* Retrieved from http://articles.latimes.com/2014/jan/29/business/la-fi-mo-target-data-breach-vendor-20140129

Independent Youth Conference, UNC-Charlotte, February 14, 2014. http://independentyouth.org/teen-network/#.

Johnson, M. T. (2011). *The diversity code: Unlock the secrets to making differences work in the real world.* New York: American Management Association.

Jue, A. L., Marr, J. A., & Kassotakis, M. E. (2010). *Social media at work: How networking tools propel organizational performance.* San Francisco: Jossey-Bass.

Kelley, T., & Kelley, D. (2012). Reclaim your creative confidence. *Harvard Business Review, 90*(12), 115–118.

Lopez, H. L. (2014). *"A growing share of Latinos get their news in English."* Retrieved from(http://www.pewhispanic.org/2013/07/23/a-growing-share-of-latinos-get-their-news-in-English/; Pp.1–4).

John C. Maxwell. "Brainy Quotes" (July 16, 2016). Retrieved from http://www.brainyquote.com/quotes/quotes/j/johncmaxw451128.html

McCrindle, M., & Wolfinger, E. (2009). *The ABC of XYZ: Understanding the global generations.* New South Wales: UNSW Press.

Mickelson, R. A. (2014). The social science evidence on the effects of diversity in K-12 schools. In C. A. Hartman (Ed.), *America's growing inequality: The impact of poverty & race* (pp. 271–274). Lanham, MD: Lexington Books.

Moskin, J. "After Slurs, Food Network Won't Renew Paula Deen. New York Times, Dining & Wine. June 21, 2013, B1.

Ortberg, J. (2003). *Everybody's normal till you get to know them.* Grand Rapids, MI: Zondervan.

Pearson, M. (2012, November 14). The Petraeus affair: A lot more than sex. CNN. Retrieved from http://www.cnn.com/2012/11/12/us/petraeus-cia-resignation

Pegues, D. (2005). 30 days to taming your tongue: What you say (and don't say) will improve your relationships. Eugene, OR: Harvest House.

Pincott, J. (2012, November 5). What's in a face? *Psychology Today.* Retrieved from https://www.psychologytoday.com/articles/201211/whats-in-face

Pink, D. H. (2005). *A whole new mind: Why right brainers will rule the future.* New York: Penguin.

Quart, A. (Narrator). (2013). *From Gen X to Z: Teens and the new cool* [documentary]. Frontline. Available from http://www.pbs.org/wgbh/frontline/article/alissa-quart-from-gen-x-to-z-teens-and-the-new-cool.

RACE – *Are We So Different?.* (2016 Exhihition). Retrieved from www.understandingrace.org.

Rapaille, C. (2006). *The culture code: An ingenious way to understand why people around the world buy and live as they do.* New York: Broadway Books.

Reyes-Chow, B. (2012, October 1). "Why do all Asians look the same?" *Huffington Post.* Retrieved from http://www.huffingtonpost.com/bruce-reyeschow/asians-look-the-same_b_1726407.html

Ropeik, D. (2010). *How risky is it, really? Why our fears don't always match the facts*. New York: McGraw-Hill.

Rosenthal, R., Hall, J. A., DiMatteo, M. R., Rogers, P. L., & Archer, D. (1979). *Sensitivity to nonverbal communication: The PONS test*. Baltimore: Johns Hopkins University Press.

Ruskoff, D. (Narrator). (2014). *Generation like* [documentary]. Frontline. Available from http://www.pbs.org/wgbh/frontline/film/generation-like

Schramski, T. (2013). The value of face-to-face communication. Retrieved from http://www.helpguide.org/articles/relationships/effective-communication.htm

Sherwood, B. (2009). *The survivors club: The secrets and science that could save your life*. New York: Hachette.

Smiley, T. (2011a). *China—The Hip-Hop Culture* [interview]. PBS. Available from http://www.pbs.org/wnet/tavissmiley/interviews/china-%E2%80%93-the-hip-hop-culture

Smiley, T. (2011b). *Jump to China* [Interview]. PBS. Available from http://www.pbs.org/wnet/tavissmiley/interviews/china-the-hip-hop-culture

Sourcewatch.(2015). Arab Spring. Retrieved from http://www.sourcewatch.org/index.php/Arab_Spring

Tapscott, D. (2009). *Grown up digital: How the Net Generation is changing your world*. New York: McGraw-Hill.

Taylor, J. B. (2006). *My stroke of insight: A brain scientist's personal journey*. New York: Penguin.

Taylor, P. (2013, November 25). When Black and White turn grey. *Sports Illustrated*. Retrieved from http://www.si.com/vault/2013/11/25/106400025/when-black-and-white-turn-gray

Tong, R. (2011). Multicultural and global feminisms. In B. J. Bank (Ed.), *Gender and higher education* (pp. 71–77). Baltimore: Johns Hopkins University Press.

Turkle, S. (2011). *Alone together: Why we expect more from technology and less from each other*. New York: Basic Books. (pp. 180–181).

US News & World Report. (2011). Rewiring your decision-making. In *Secrets of your brain* (pp. 23–25). Washington, DC: Author.

Voss, G. (2013, March 1). Why we're born to judge. *Women's Health*. Retrieved from http://www.womenshealthmag.com/life/prejudiceweird. (n.d.). In *Merriam-Webster*. Retrieved from http://www.merriam-webster.com/dictionary/weird

White, T. (2013, November 2). Why social media isn't social. *Huffington Post*. Retrieved from http://www.huffingtonpost.com/thomas-white/why-social-media-isnt-social_b_3858576.html

Winant, H. (2007). *The world is a ghetto*. New York: Basic Books.

Wise, T. (2010). *Colorblind: The rise of post-racial politics and the retreat from racial equity*. San Francisco: City Lights Books.

Wortmann, C. (2006). *What's your story? Using stories to ignite performance and be more successful*. Chicago: Kaplan.

Young, S. (2007). *Micromessaging: Why great leadership is beyond words.* New York: McGraw-Hill.

Young, S. (2007). "*Social Graces: Business Etiquette.*" Town and Country Magazine. Spring 2007.

Zachery, G.P. (2005). "Making It In China" CNN Money. Retrieved from http://money.cnn.com/magazines/business2/business2_archive/2005/08/01/8269649/inde   x.htm.

Zemke, R., Raines, C., & Filipczak, B. (2000). *Generations at work: Managing the clash of veterans, Boomers, Xers, and Nexters in your workplace.* New York: American Management Association

CPSIA information can be obtained
at www.ICGtesting.com
Printed in the USA
FSHW010115130619
59001FS